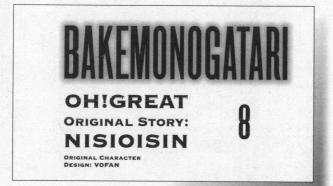

BAKEMONOGATARI

OH!GREAT

ORIGINAL STORY:
NISIOISIN

ORIGINAL CHARACTER
DESIGN: VOFAN

8

Nadeko Sengoku

A girl in the grip of a "snake." She reunites with Koyomi as she searches for a way to rid herself of the pain she suffers while under the snake's curse.

Mèmè Oshino

An expert on aberrations who has made the ruins of a former cram school his home. The man Koyomi goes to for advice whenever he happens upon an aberration.

Tsubasa Hanekawa

Koyomi's classmate who was once bewitched by a "cat." An honor student that no honor could sufficiently describe, and a class president among class presidents.

Koyomi Araragi

A boy who was attacked by a vampire. He is now working with Suruga in a desperate effort to save Nadeko, his little sister's friend, by dispelling a curse on her.

Suruga Kanbaru

A girl who made a wish to a "monkey." Though the aberration ended up remaining in her left arm, she has resolved her own problems and is now helping Koyomi out with his latest task.

Shinobu Oshino

The shadow of the vampire who once attacked Koyomi. She was given her current name by Mèmè as a way to bind her existence.

MAIN CHARACTERS

THE STORY SO FAR

Nadeko Sengoku, a girl in the grip of a "snake," was searching for a way to undo the serpent's curse that causes her suffering, but nothing was working. She is then reunited with Koyomi, the older brother of one of her elementary-school classmates. He agrees to help her, and they seem to make good progress toward dispelling the curse...but when the situation takes a sudden turn, they come to realize something: There were two "snakes."

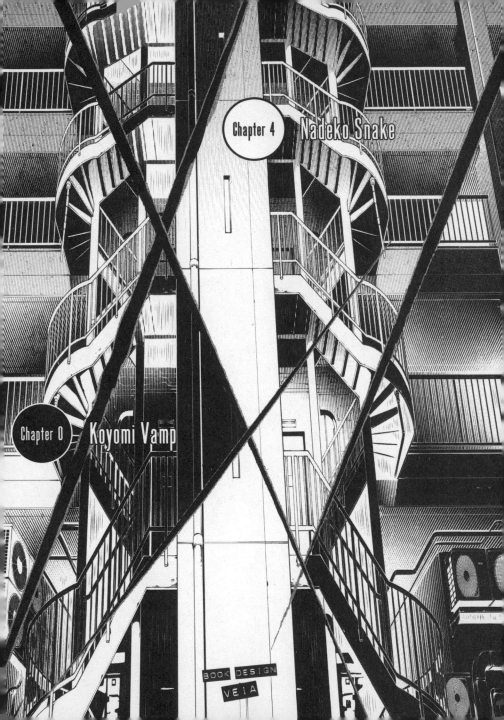

Chapter 4   Nadeko Snake

Chapter 0   Koyomi Vamp

BOOK DESIGN
VEIA

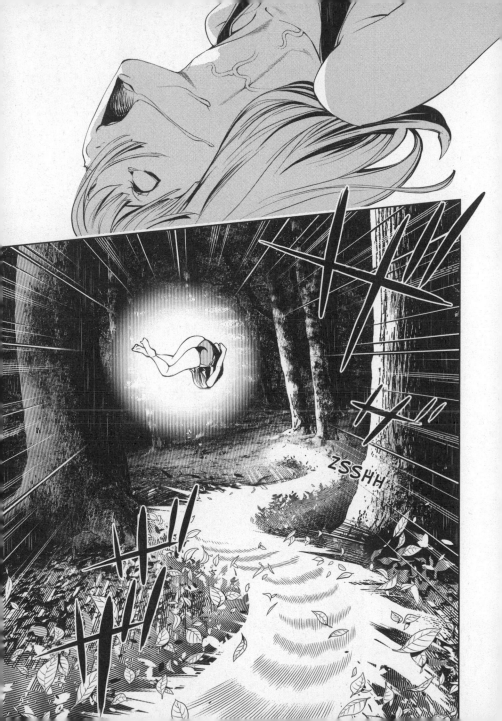

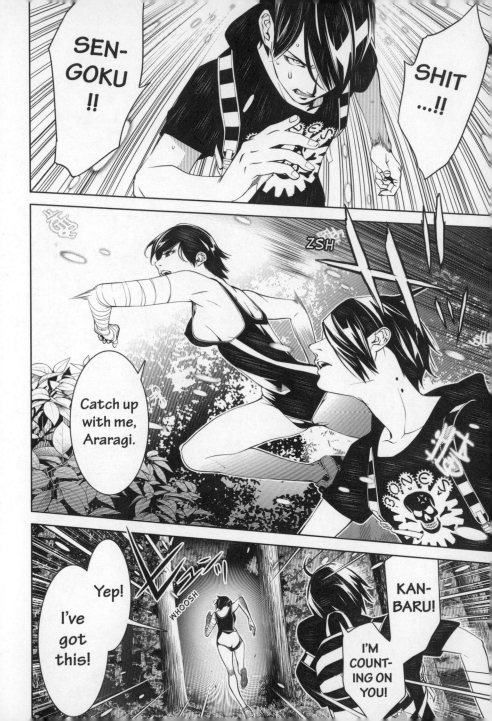

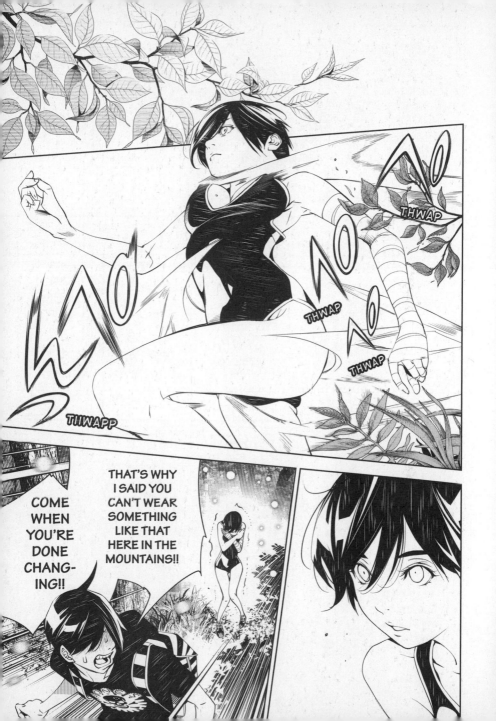

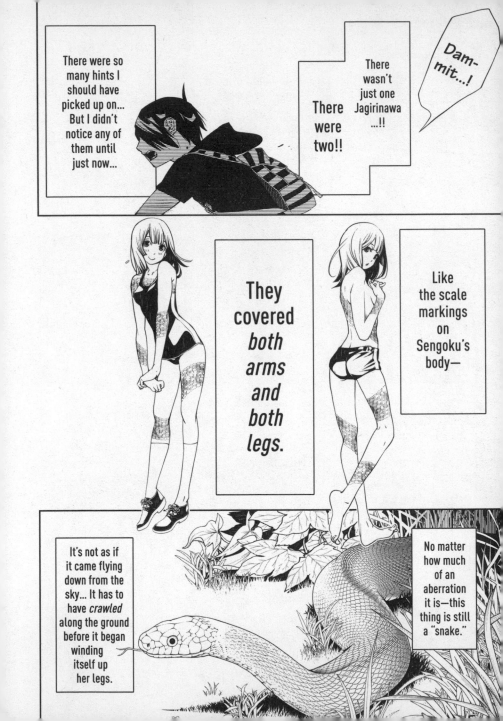

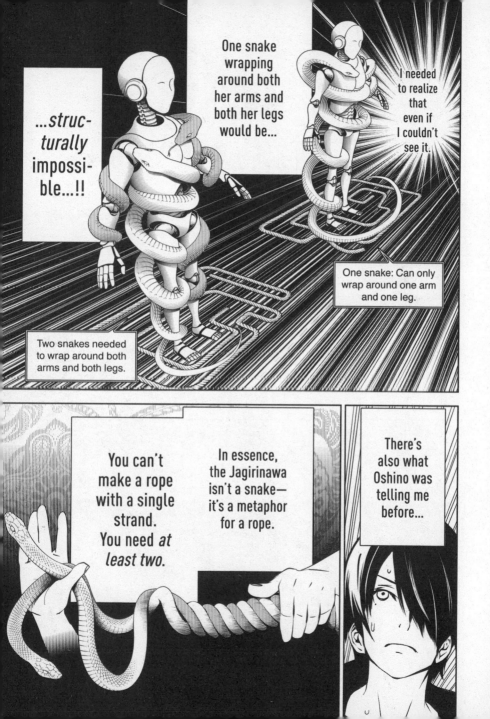

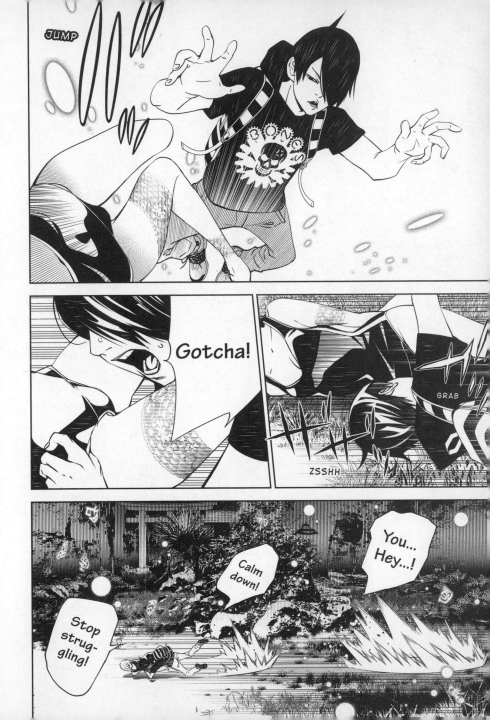

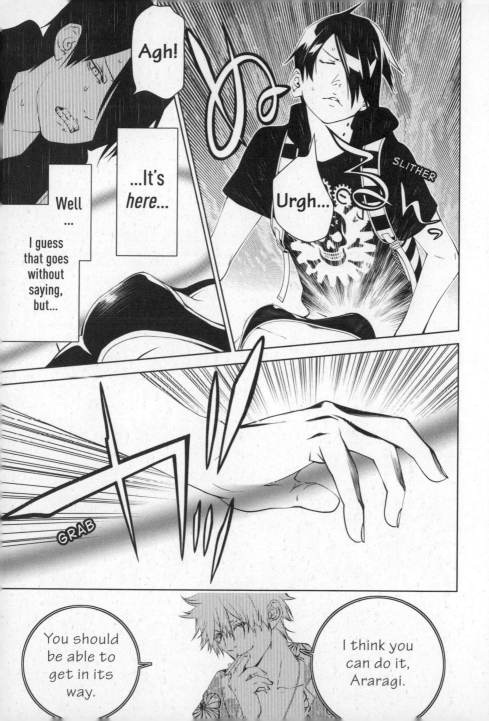

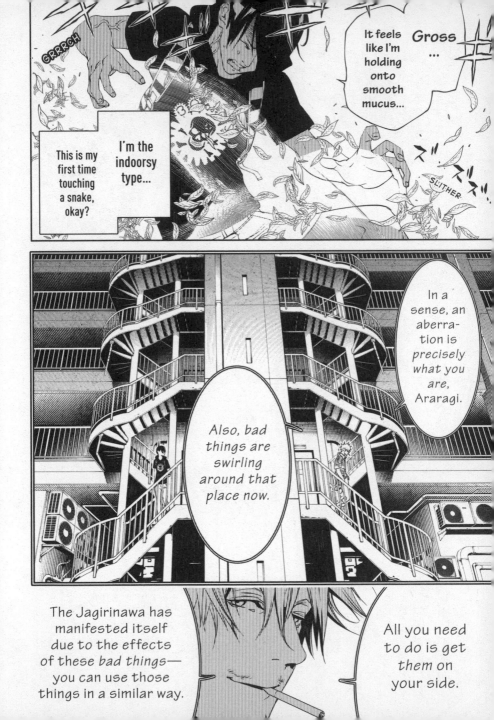

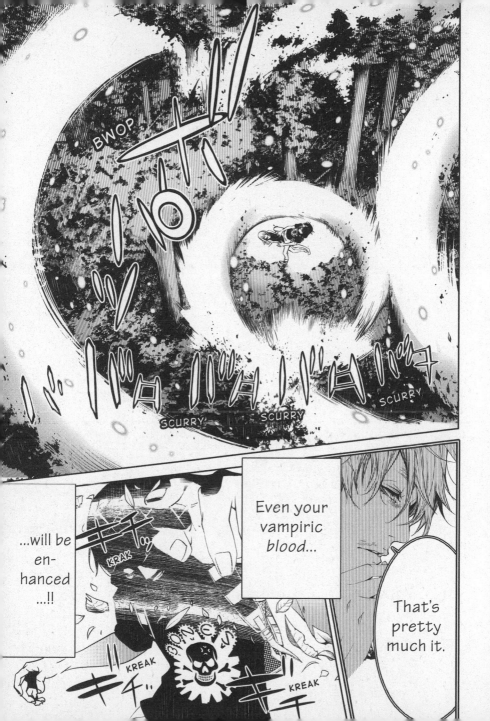

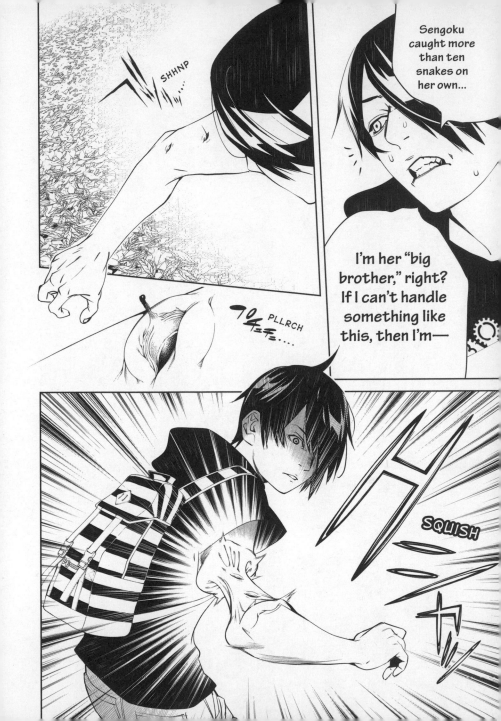

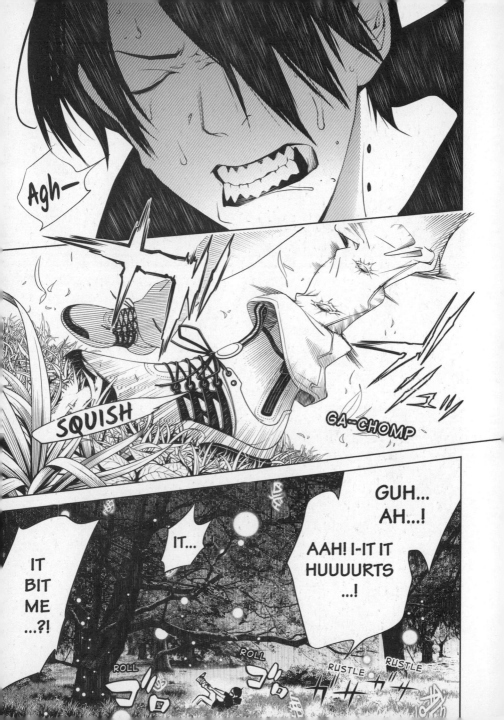

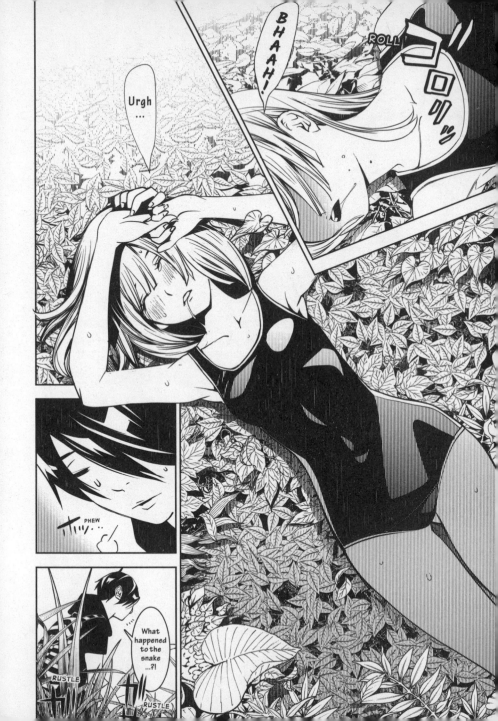

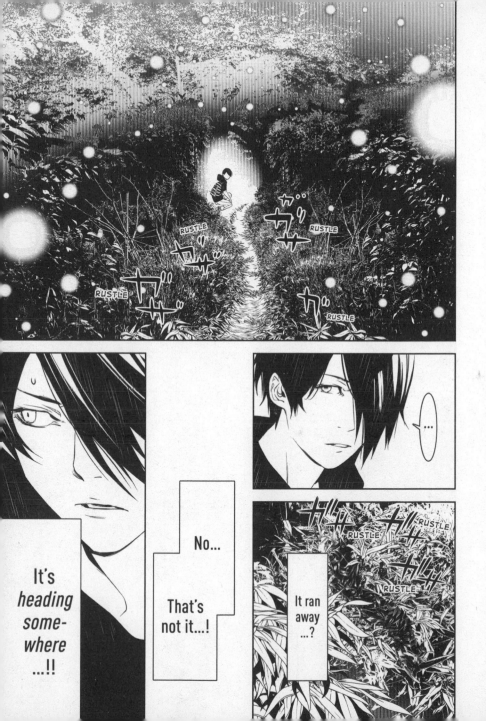

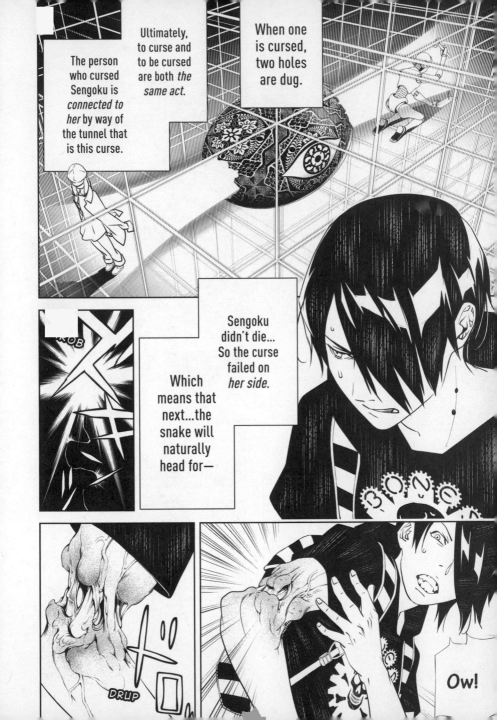

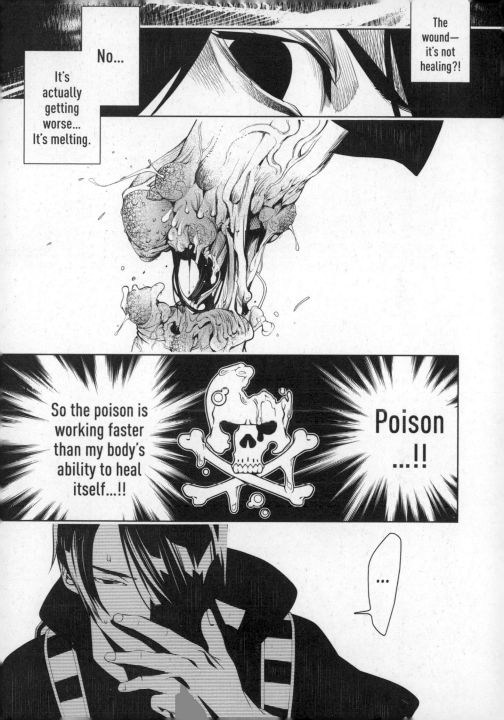

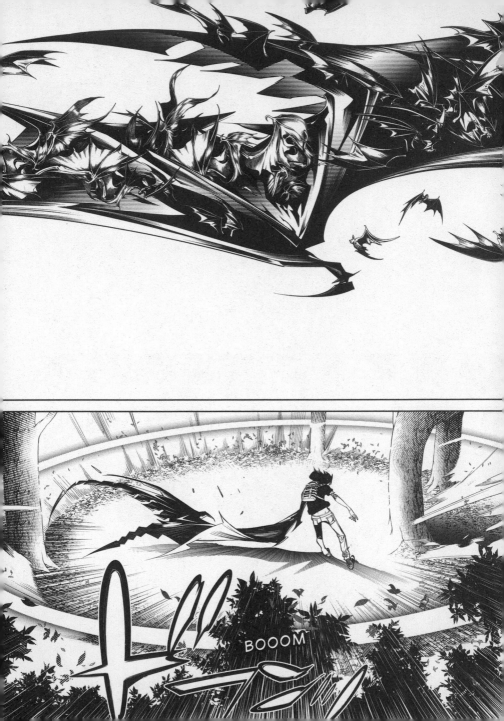

BOOOM

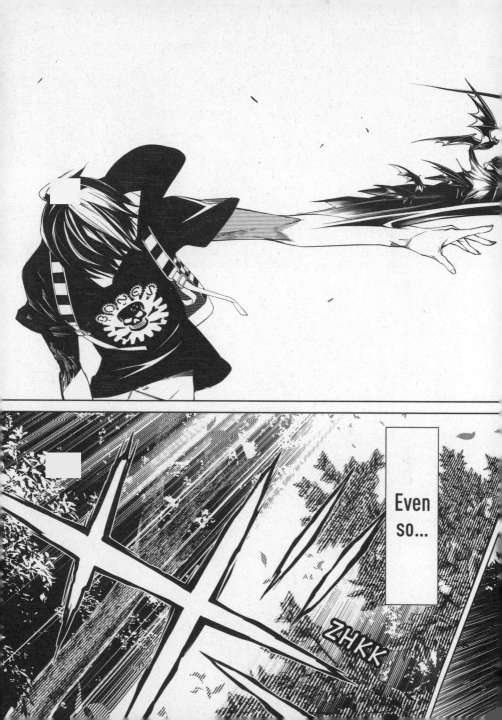

Even so...

ZHKK

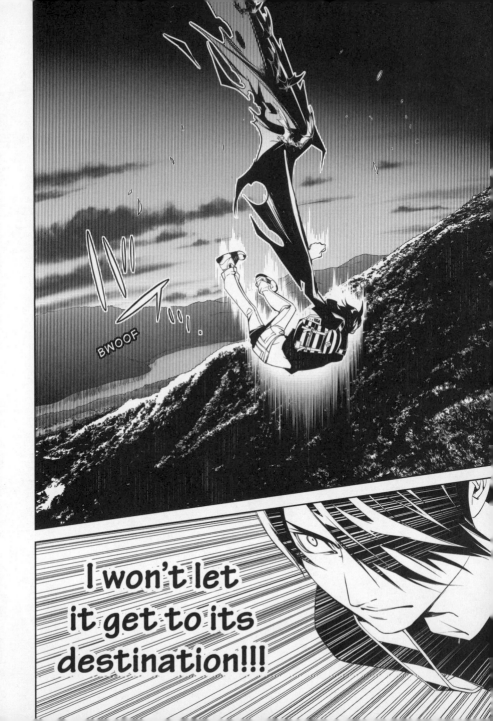

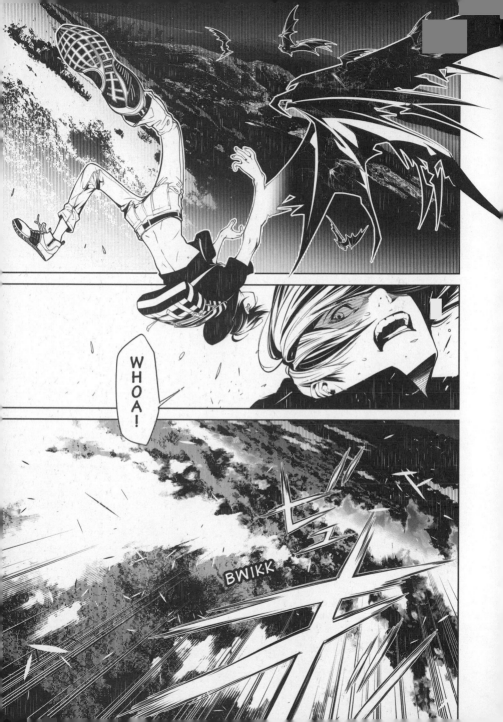

Sengoku just *happened* to know me, but it's different for this other girl— she doesn't have a single way to protect herself, and I don't see how I'll be able to save her!!

The snake is heading toward the person who cursed Sengoku.

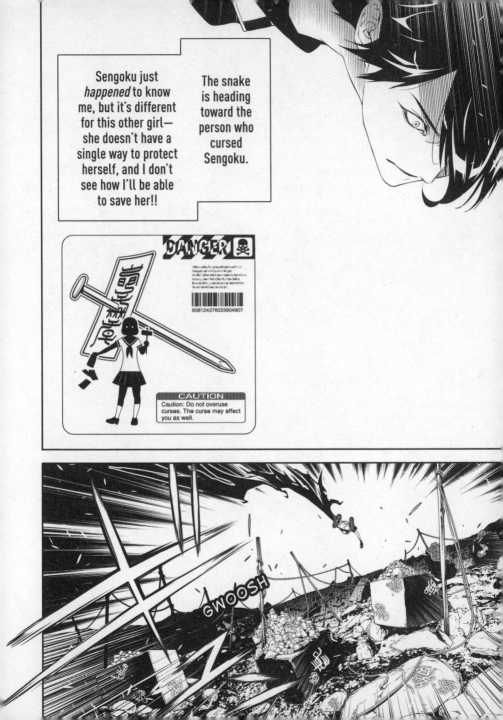

GWOOSH

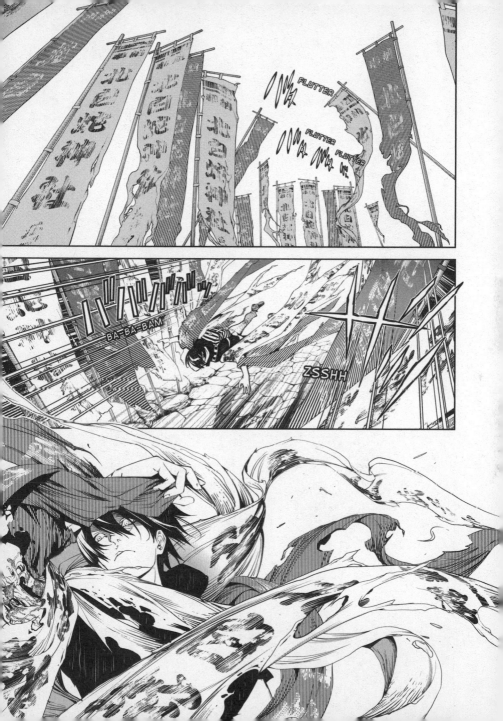

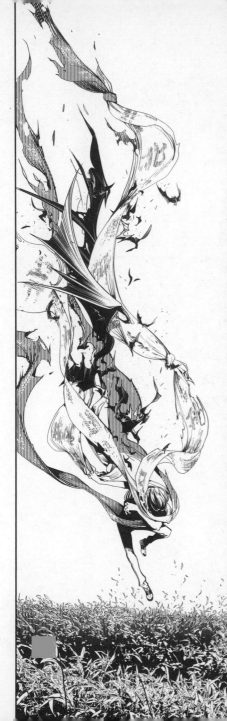

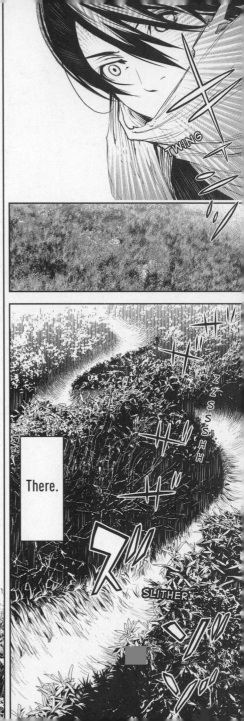

There.

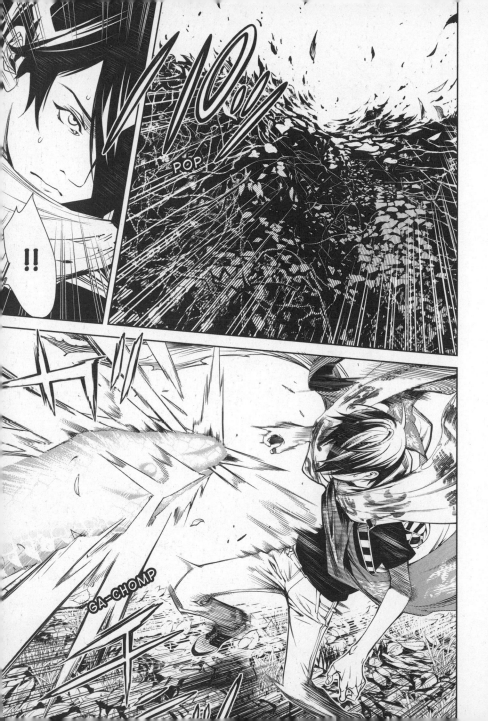

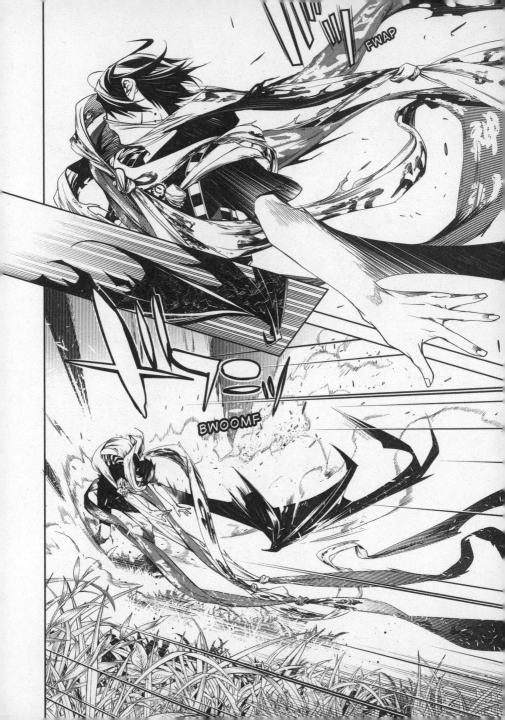

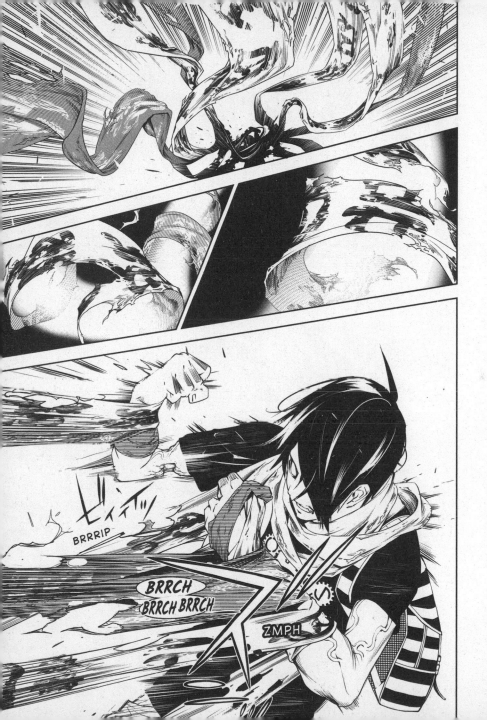

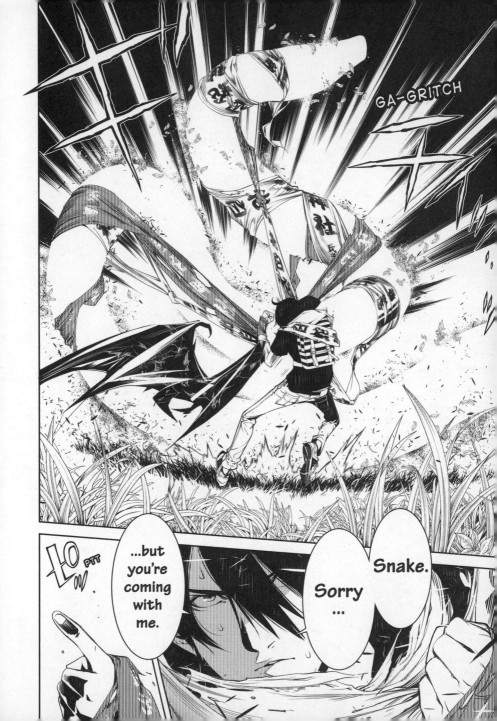

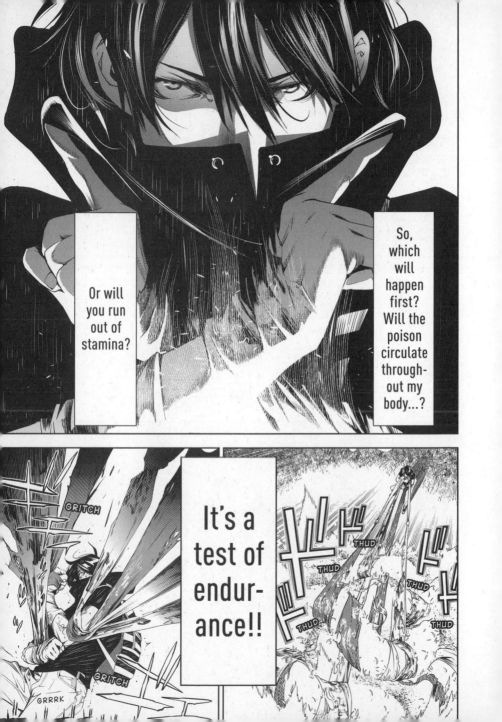

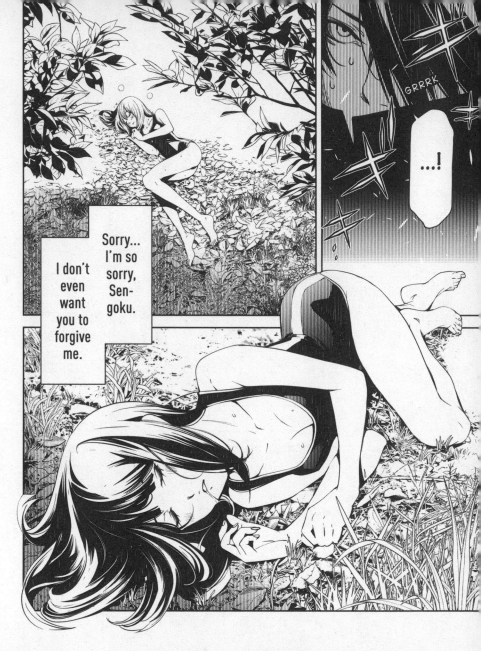

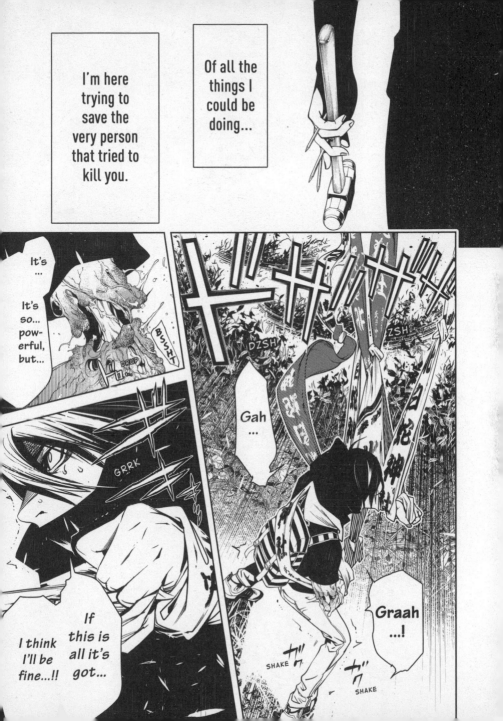

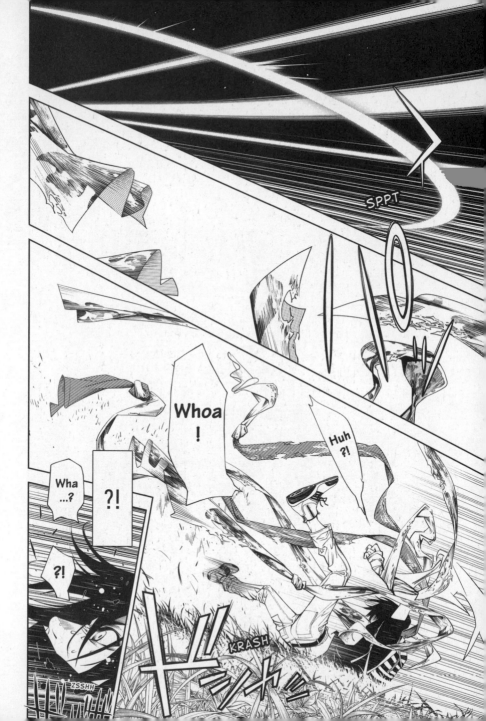

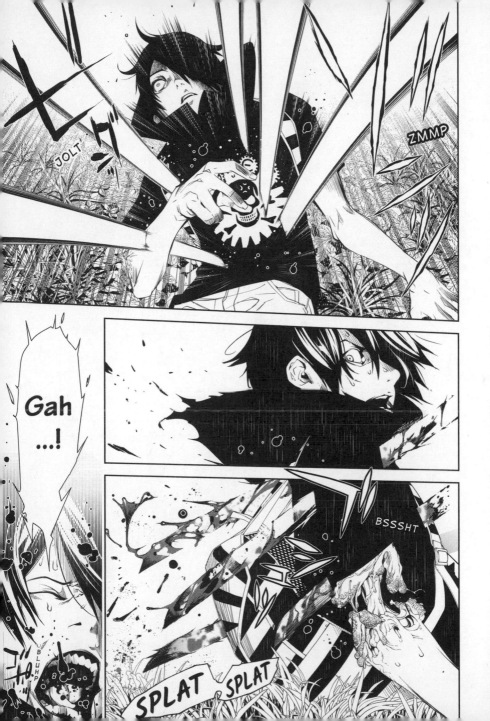

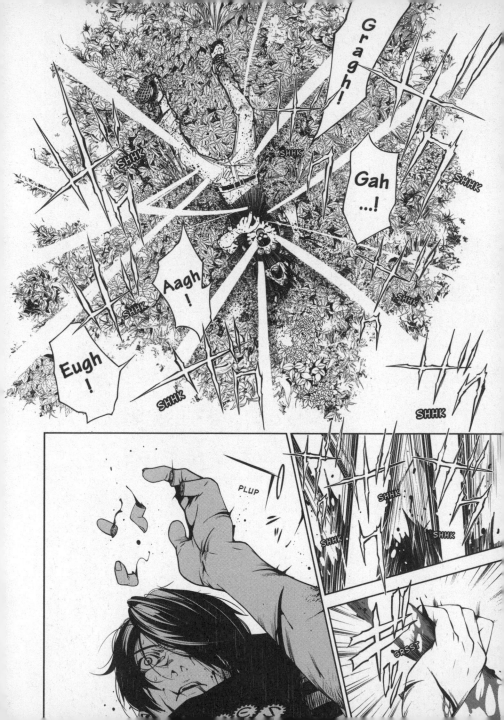

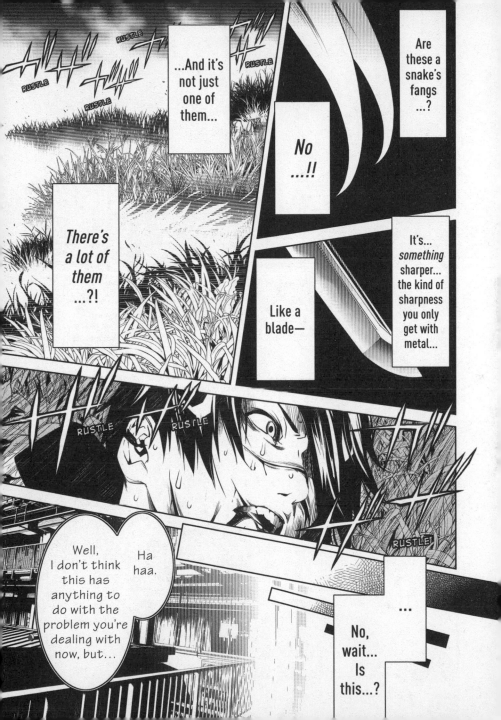

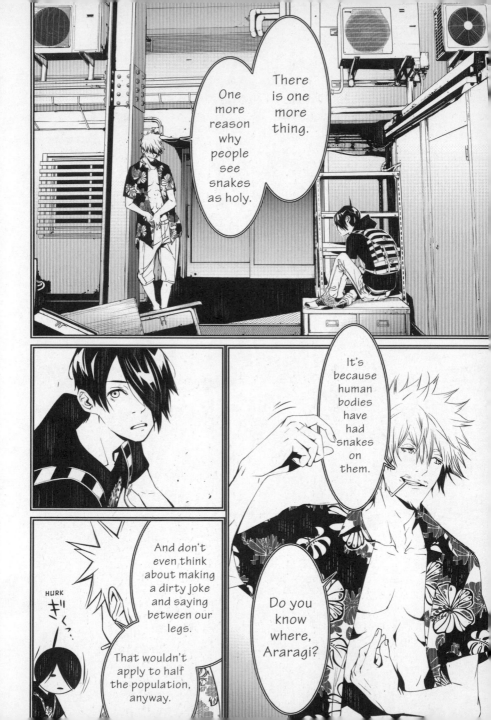

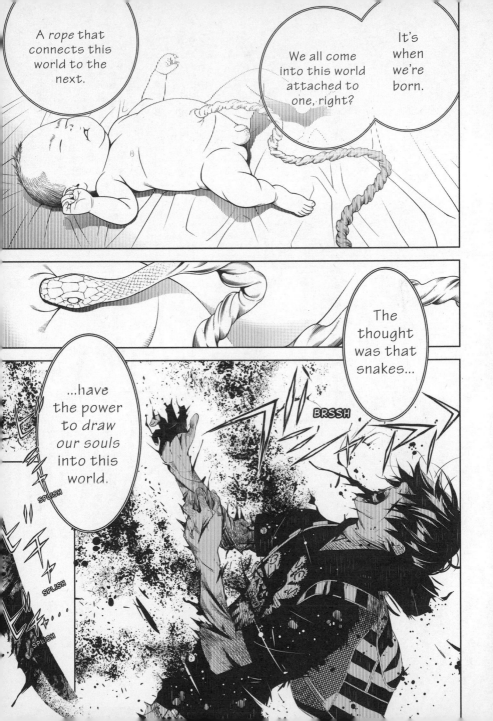

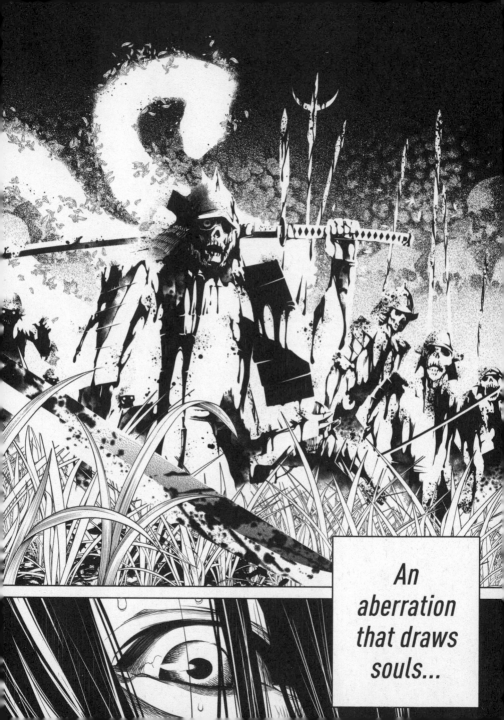

An aberration that draws souls...

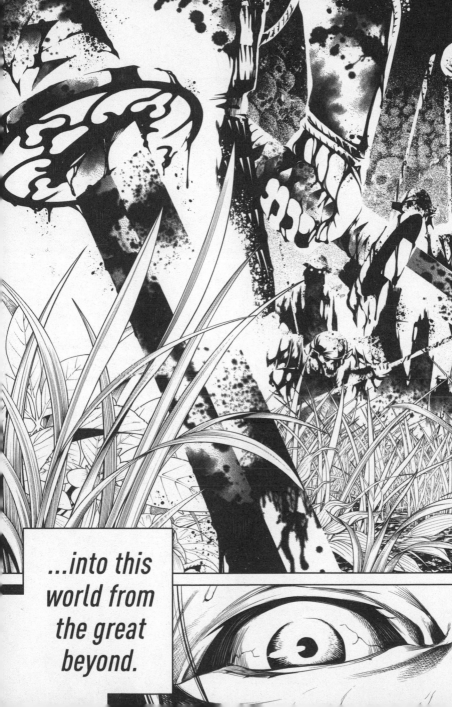

...into this world from the great beyond.

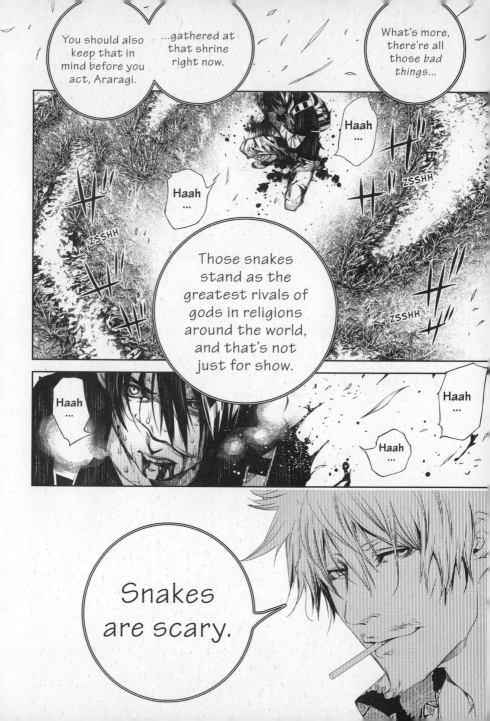

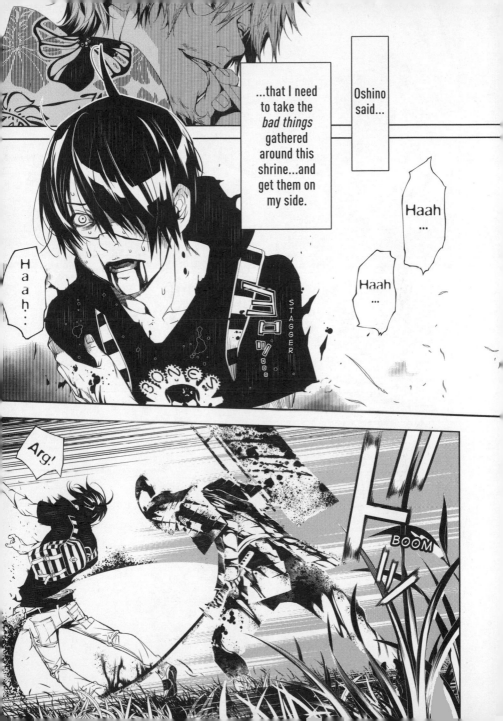

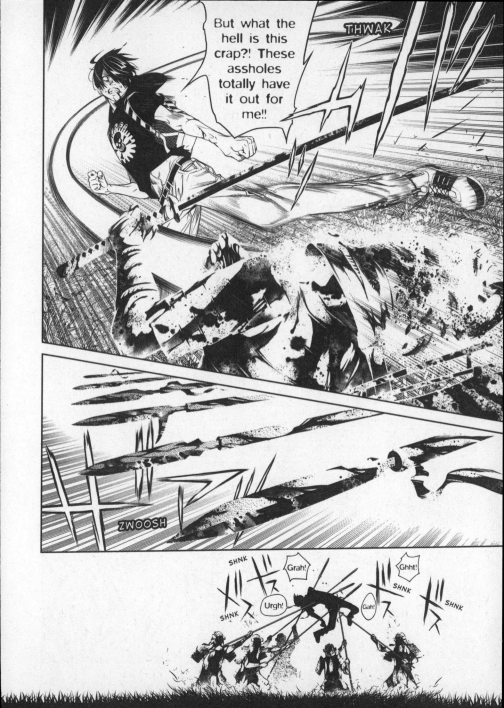

Kuh
—

Haakh
!

...You all
should
know
some-
thing,
though
...

I let
you
stab
me
just
now.

I did that
so I could
get you
jerks in
one place
even if I
can't see
you!!

SHLRRK

GRIP

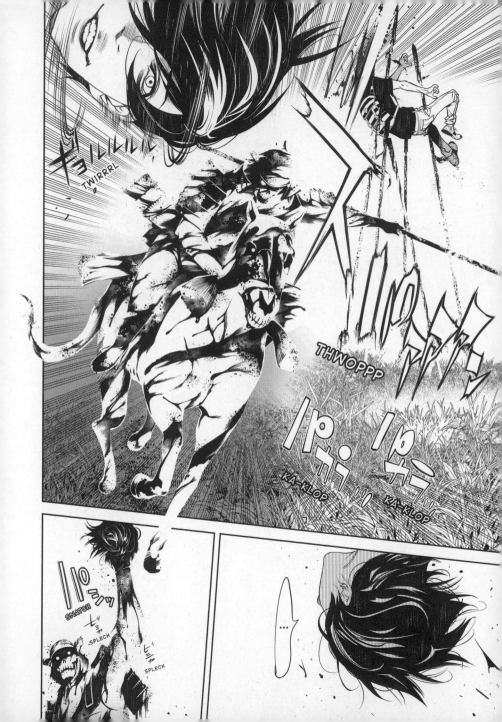

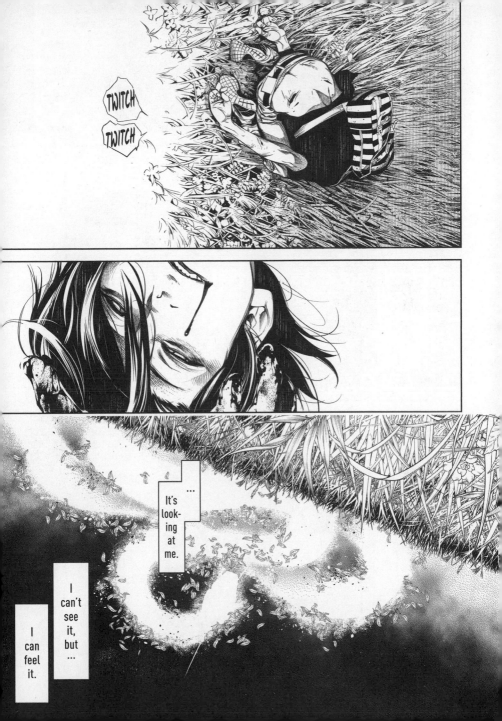

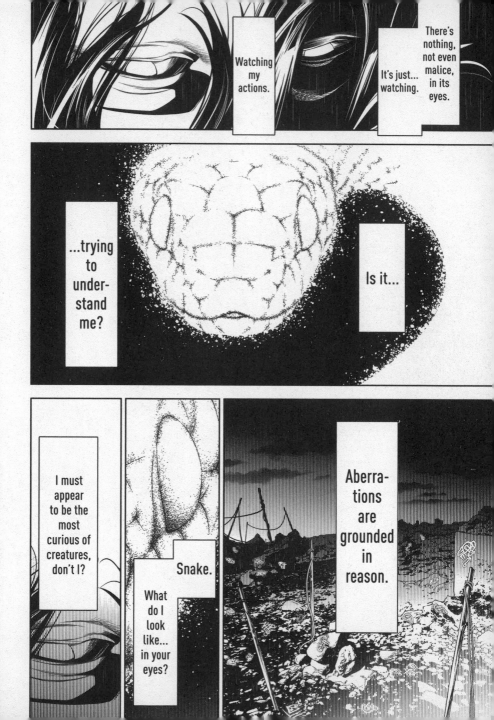

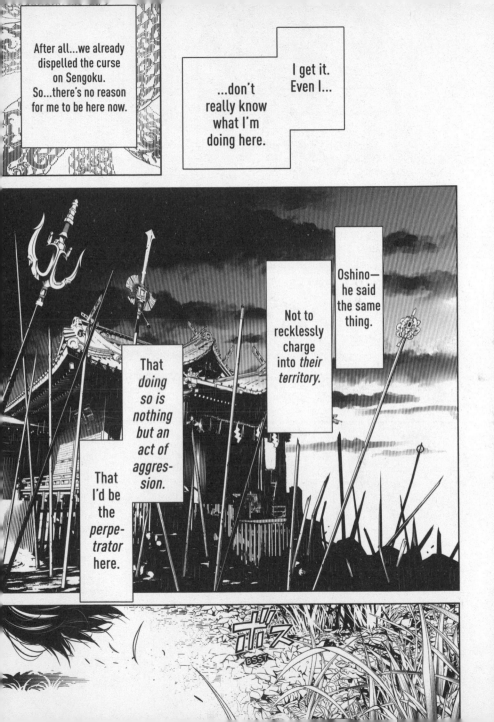

After all...we already dispelled the curse on Sengoku. So...there's no reason for me to be here now.

...don't really know what I'm doing here.

I get it. Even I...

Oshino—he said the same thing.

Not to recklessly charge into *their* territory.

That *doing so is nothing but an act of aggression.*

That I'd be the *perpetrator* here.

ガサッ
BSST

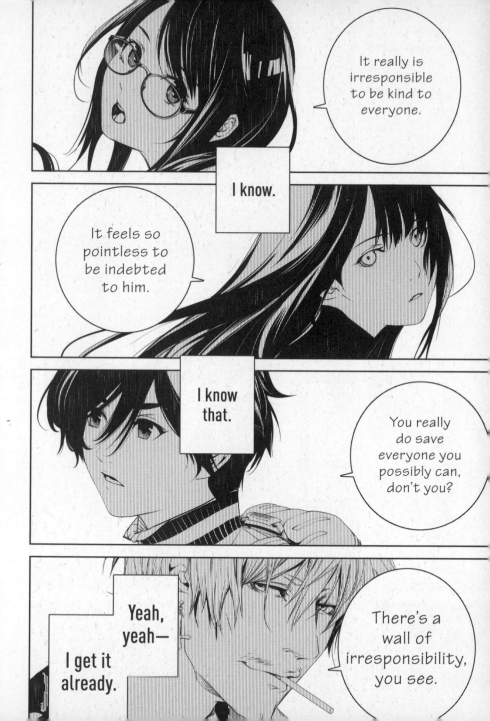

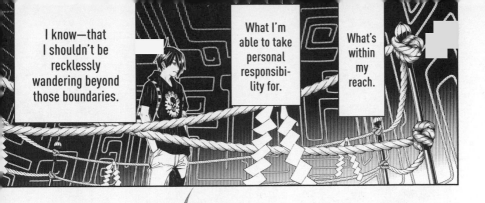

I know—that I shouldn't be recklessly wandering beyond those boundaries.

What I'm able to take personal responsibility for.

What's within my reach.

That in the end, *it's not for anyone's sake.*

I know all of that.

That saving someone when it's *not for their sake...* is nothing more than *poison.*

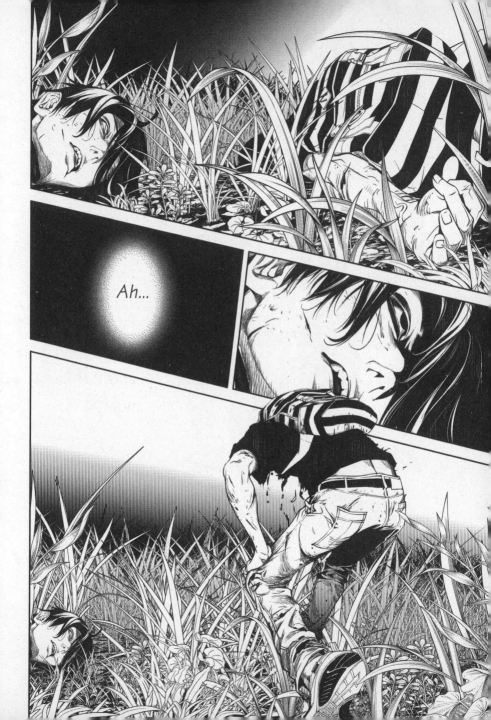

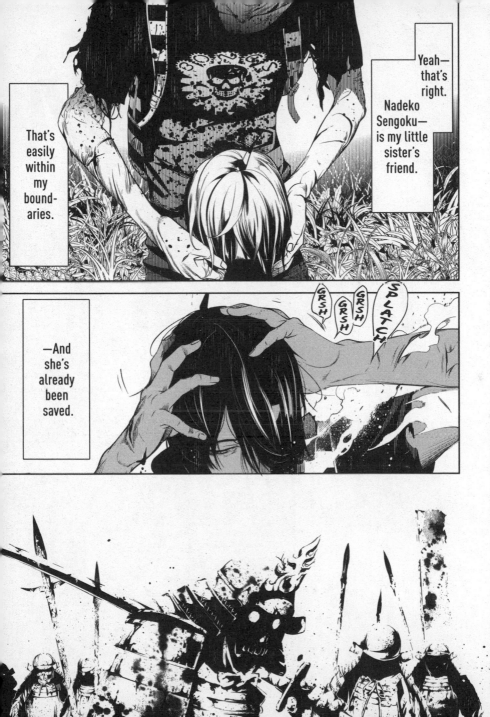

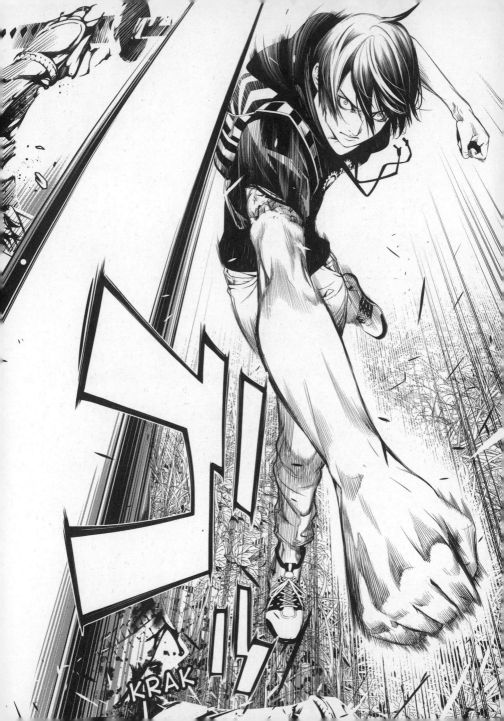

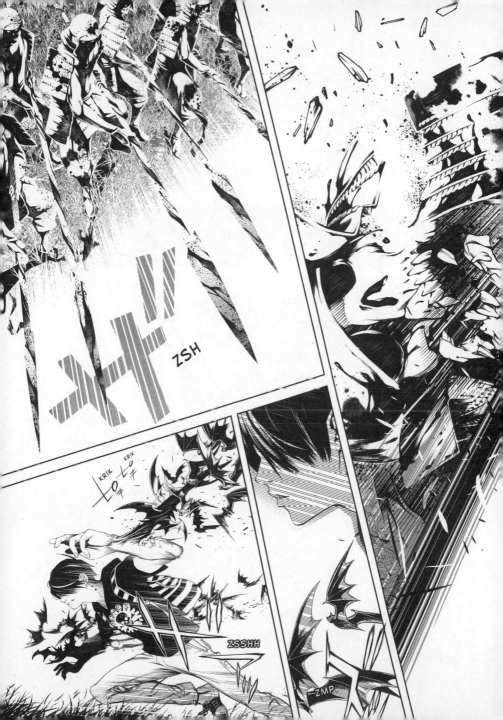

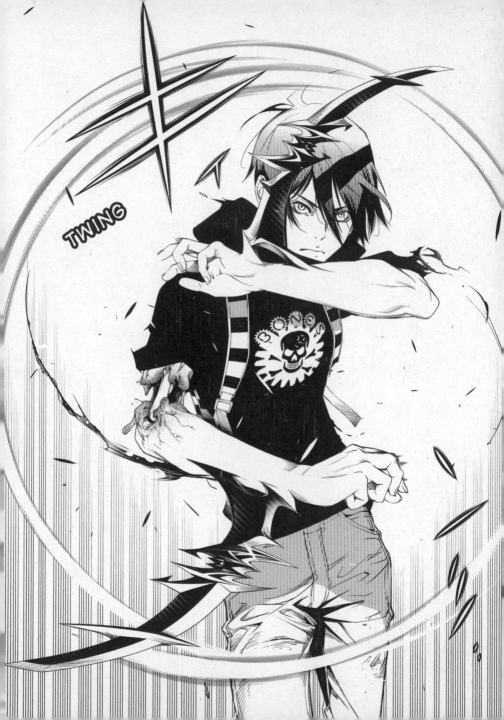

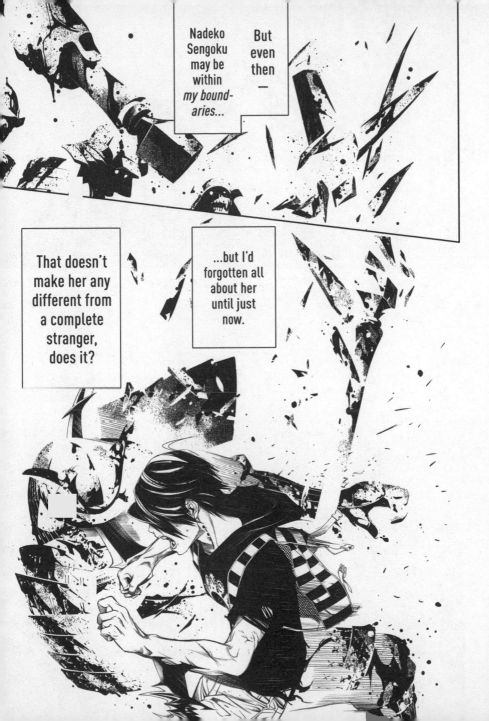

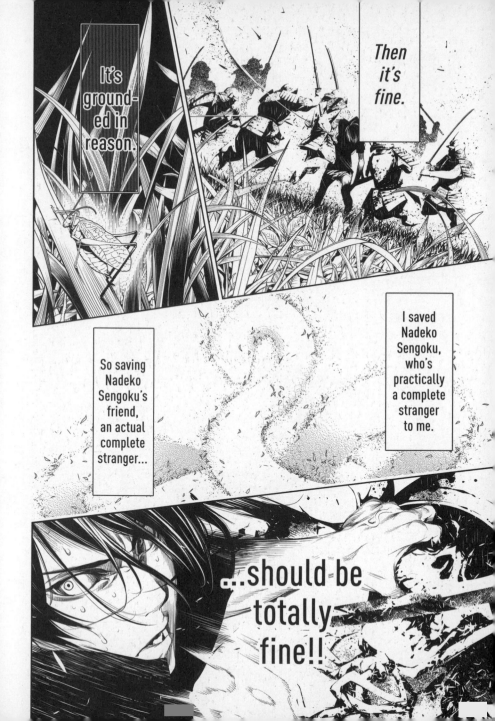

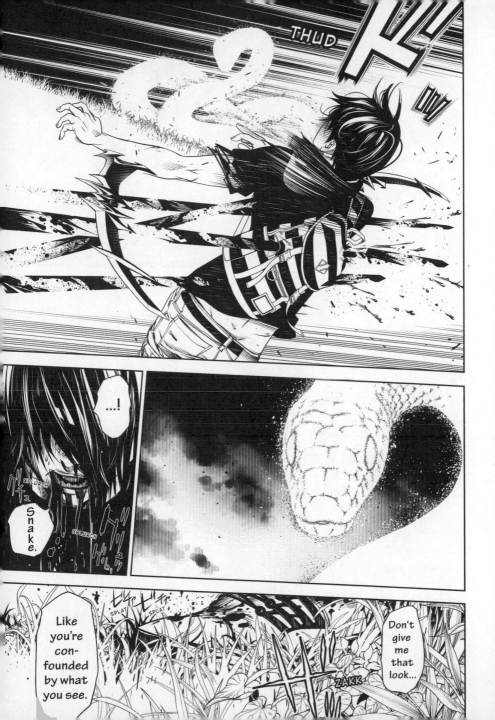

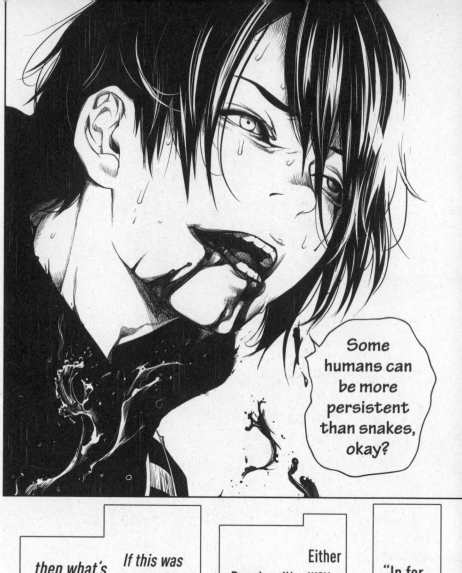

Some humans can be more persistent than snakes, okay?

then what's so wrong about going and saving someone for my own sake?

If this was never for anyone's sake to begin with,

People will go and get saved on their own.

Either way...

"In for a penny, in for a pound," right?

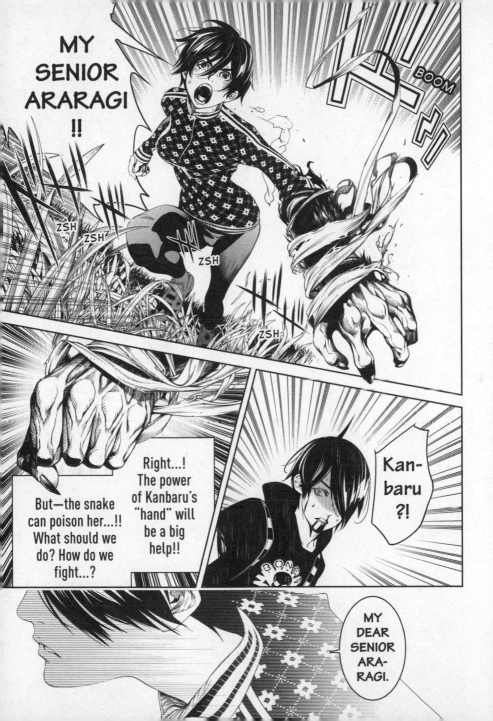

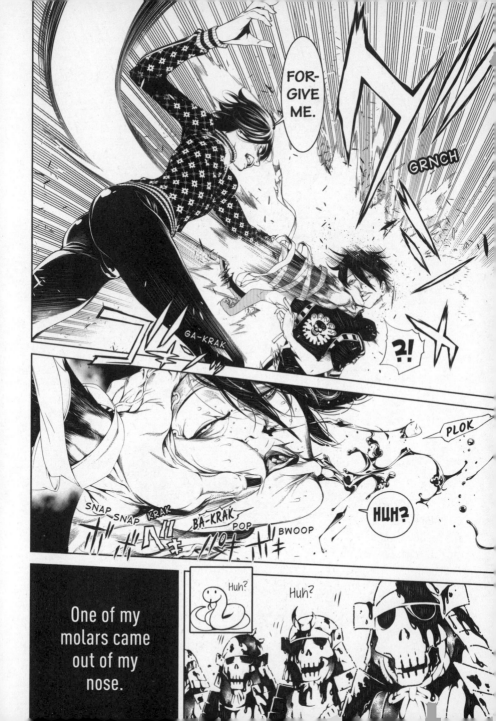

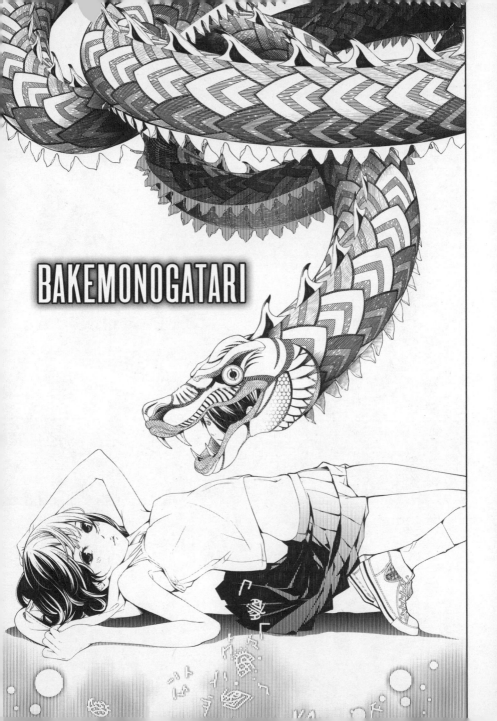

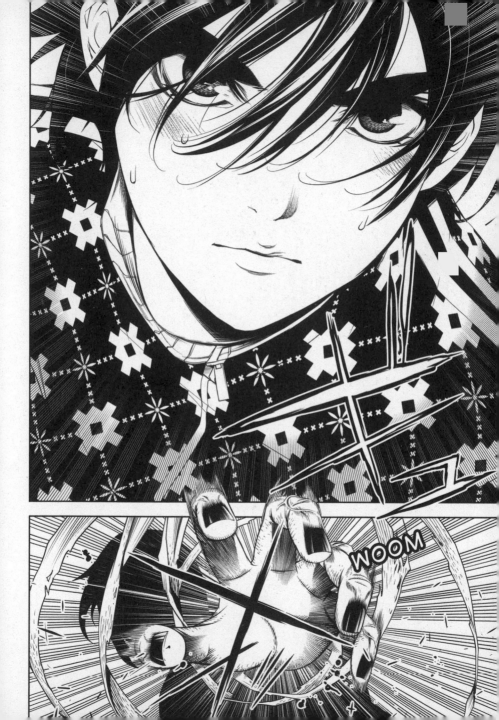

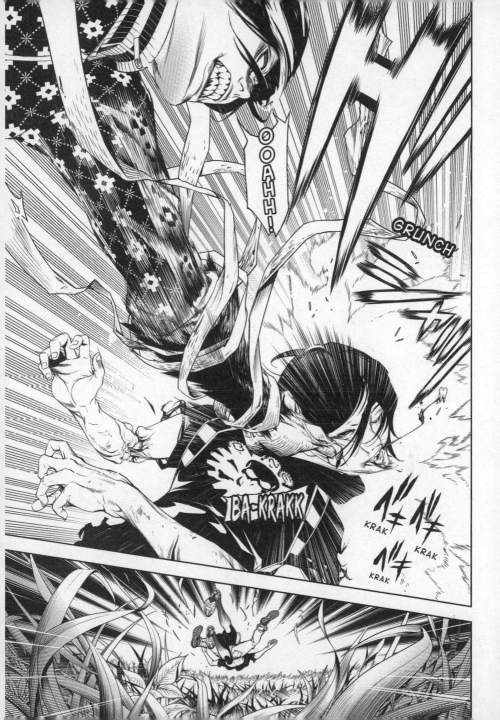

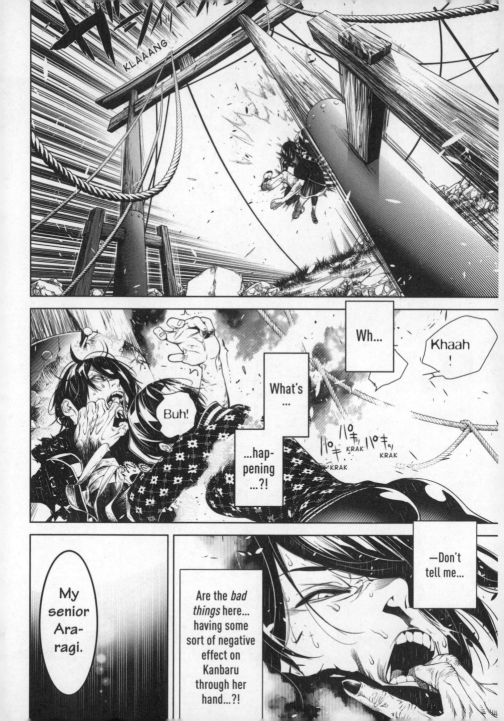

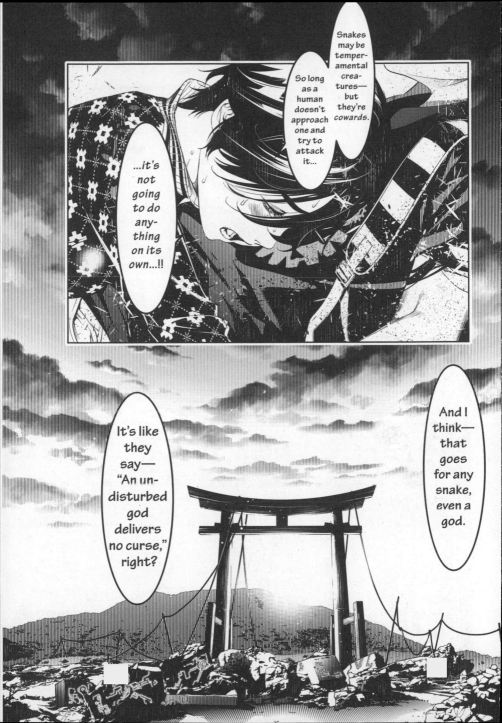

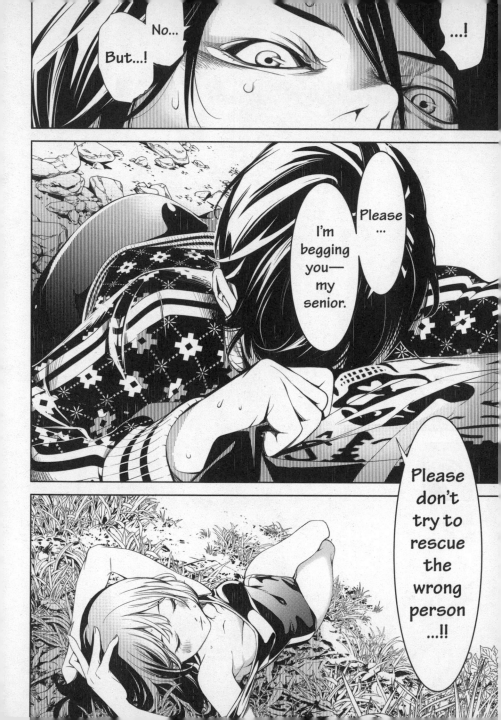

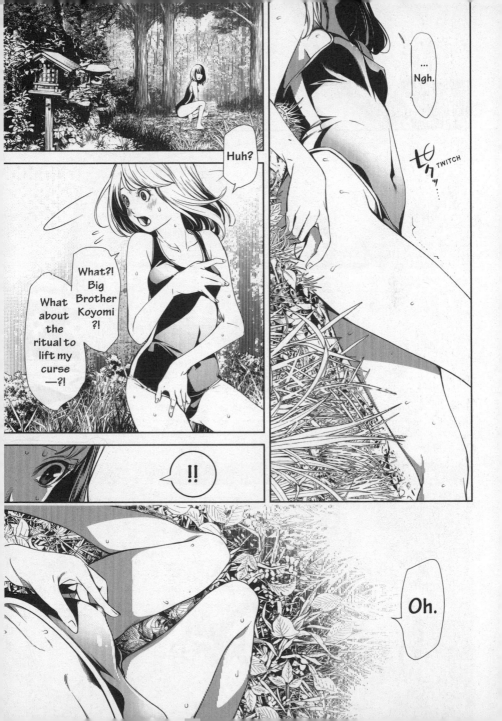

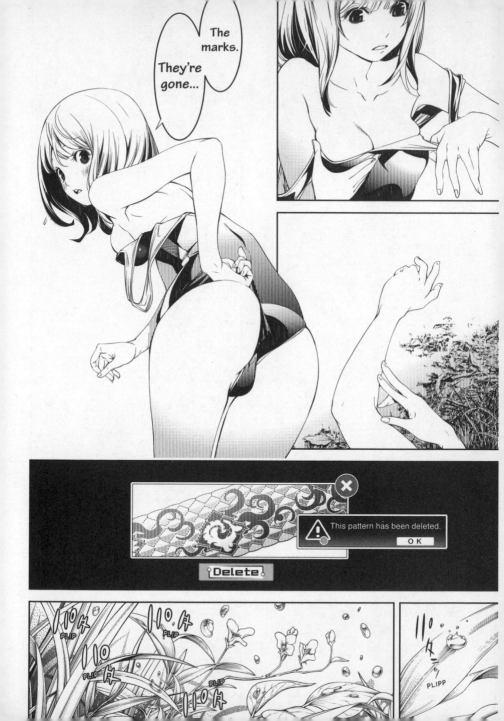

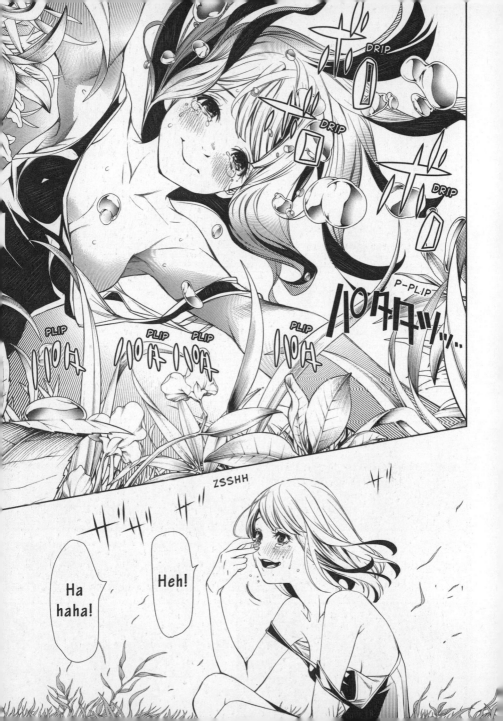

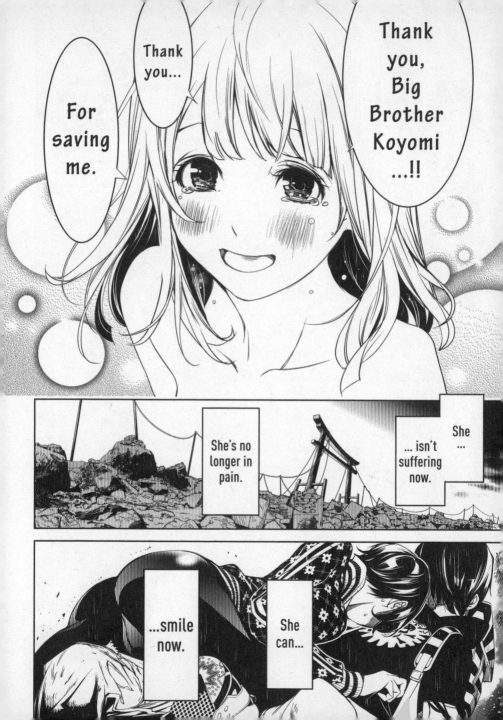

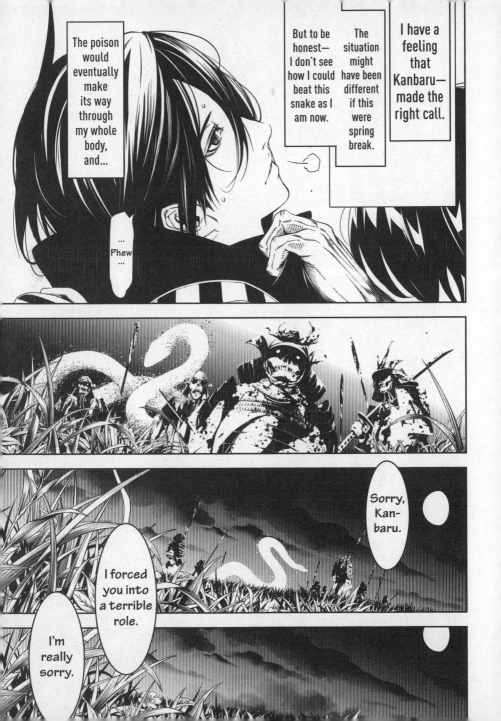

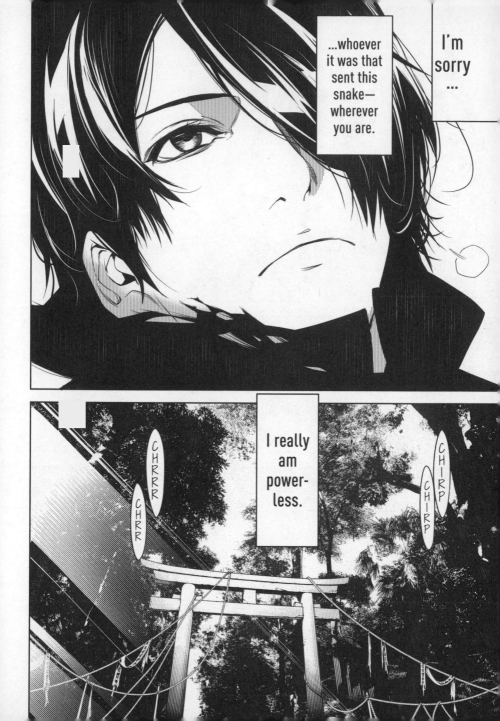

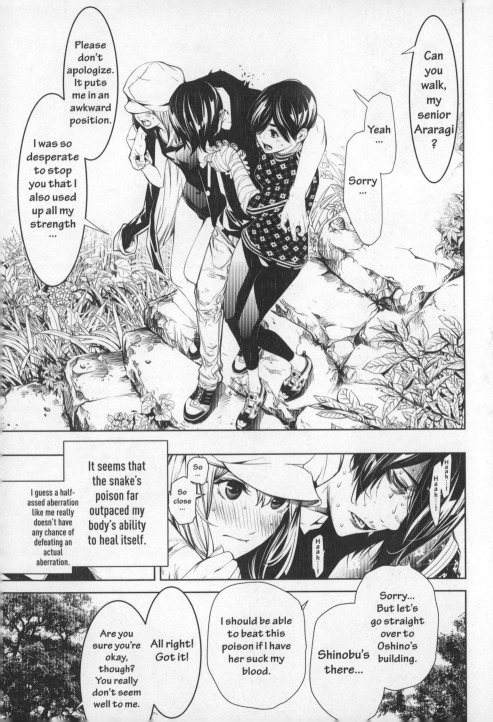

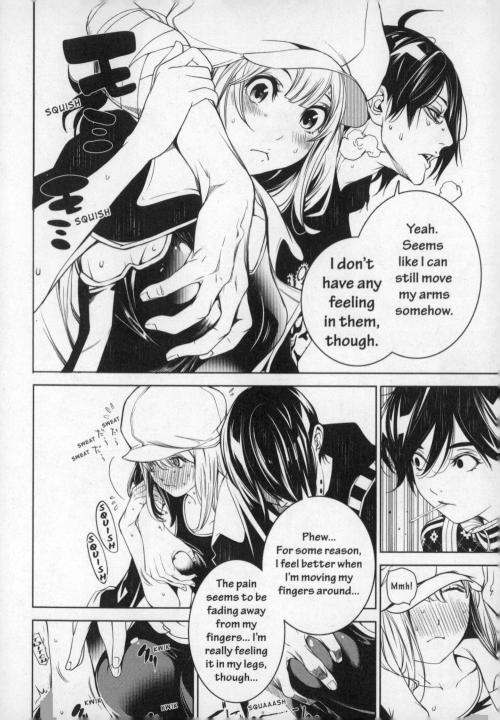

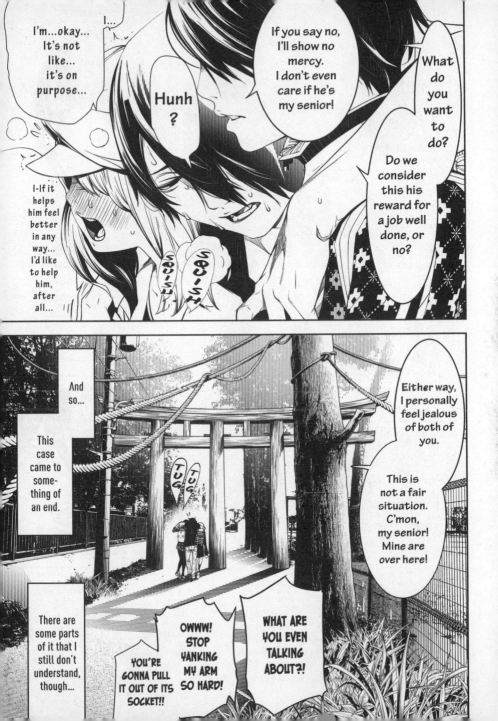

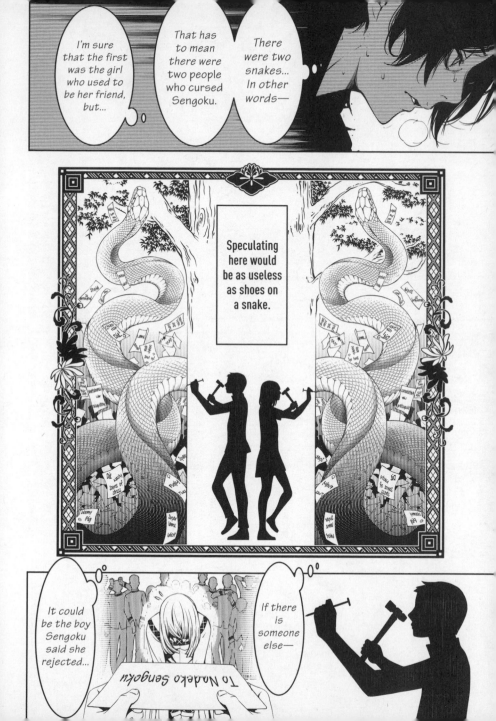

We're here, my senior Araragi. It's amazing what taxis can do.

SQUISH
SQUISH

Um... Miss Kanbaru? At first...I was told about a simpler ritual.

But then... I guess I went online to look stuff up and got deeper and deeper into it...

NO UNAUTHORIZED ENTRY PAST THIS POINT

...I'm amazed that what was basically child's play could take you out like this...

Still... Considering this was just an occult fad that was making the rounds at some school...

Kaiki.

—I think he said his name... was Mister Kaiki...

SQUISH
SQUISH
WARM
WARM

Um... What was his name again ...?

Oh... There's a man who specializes in that kind of thing.

What do you mean, you were told?

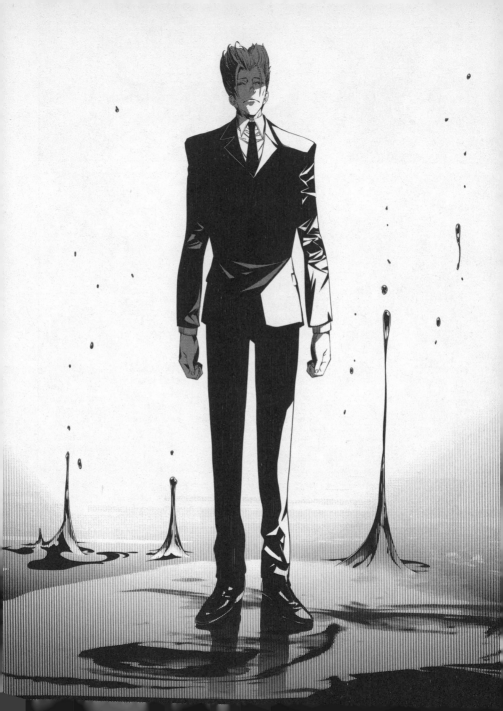

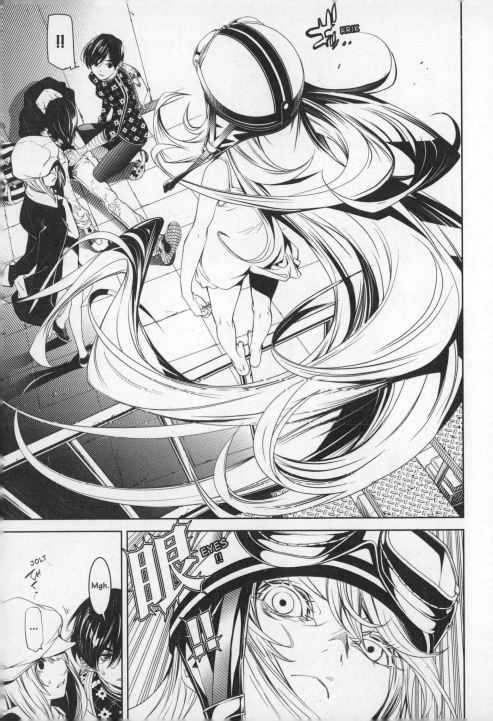

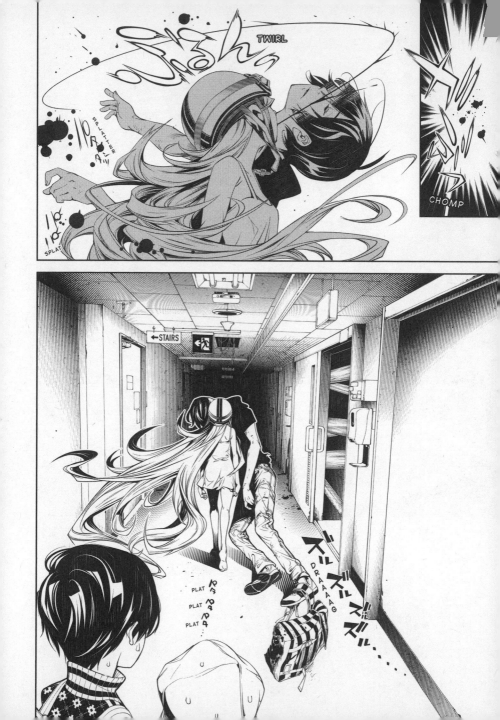

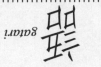

物 *mono*

語 *gatari*

$$\frac{\text{NADEKOsnake}}{8}$$

化 *bake*

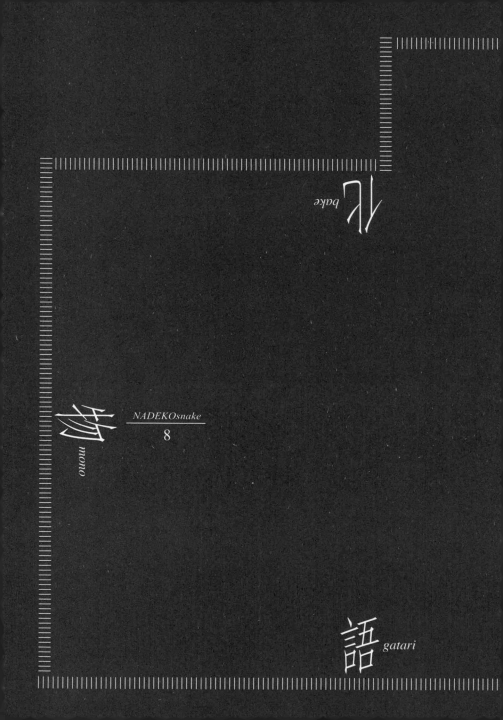

化 *bake*

物 *mono*

NADEKOsnake
8

語 *gatari*

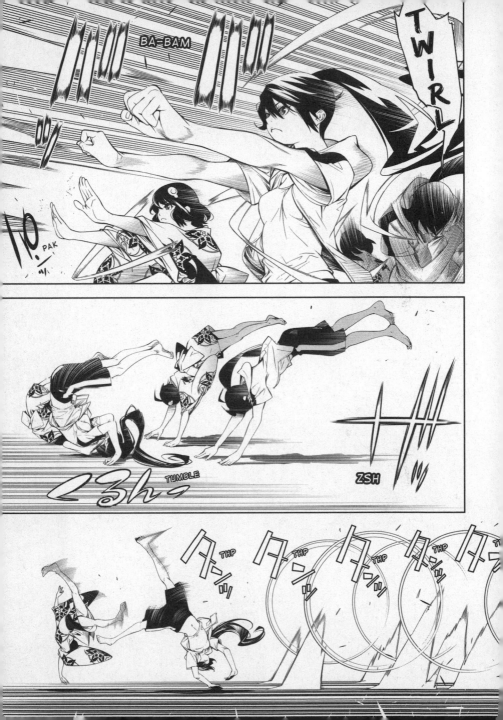

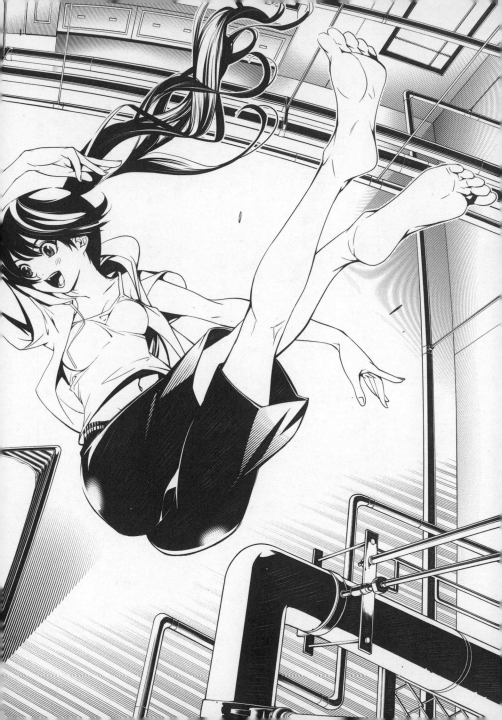

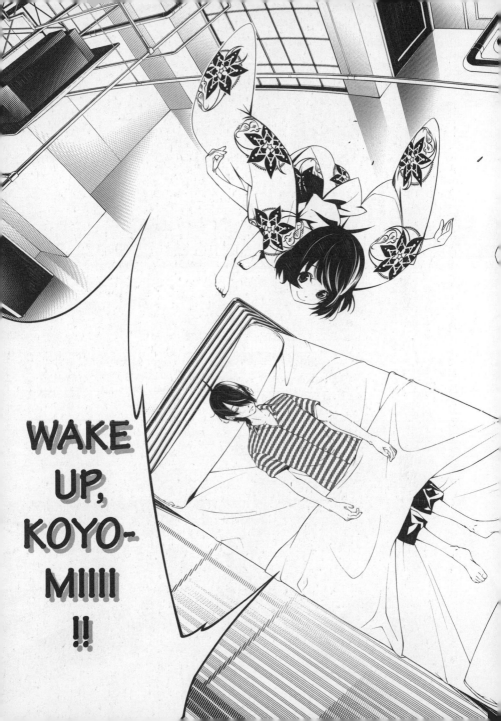

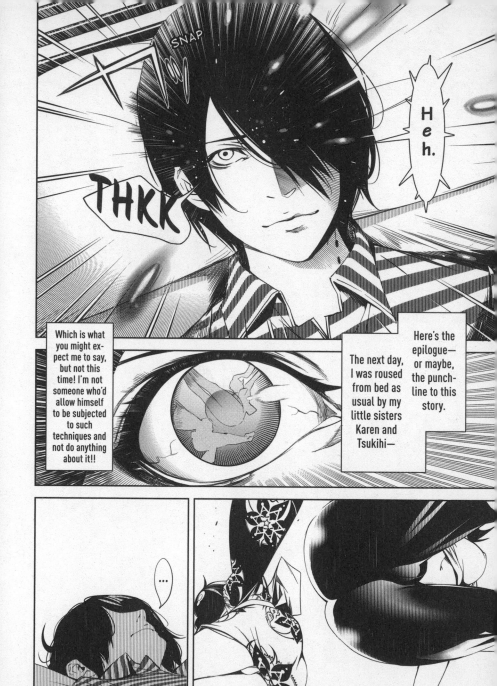

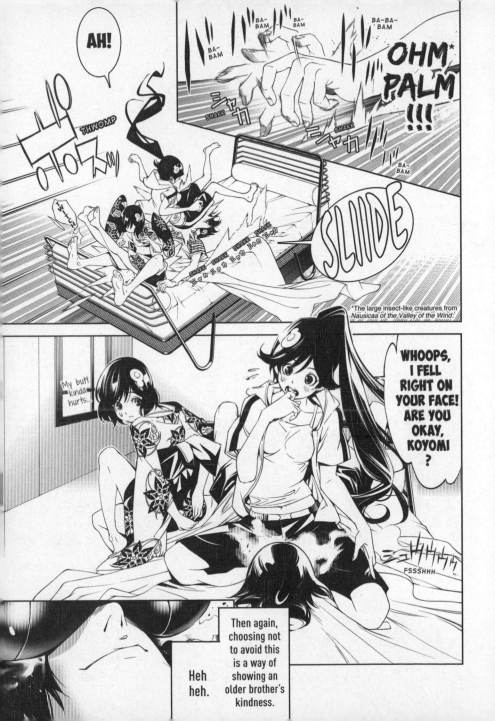

*The large insect-like creatures from 'Nausicaa of the Valley of the Wind'.

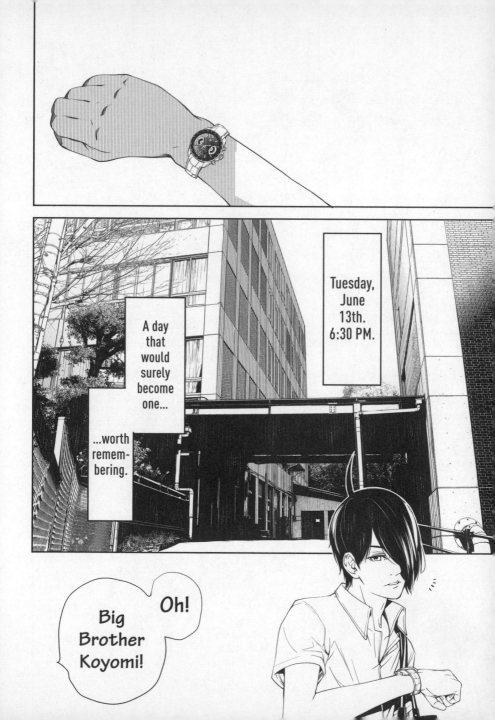

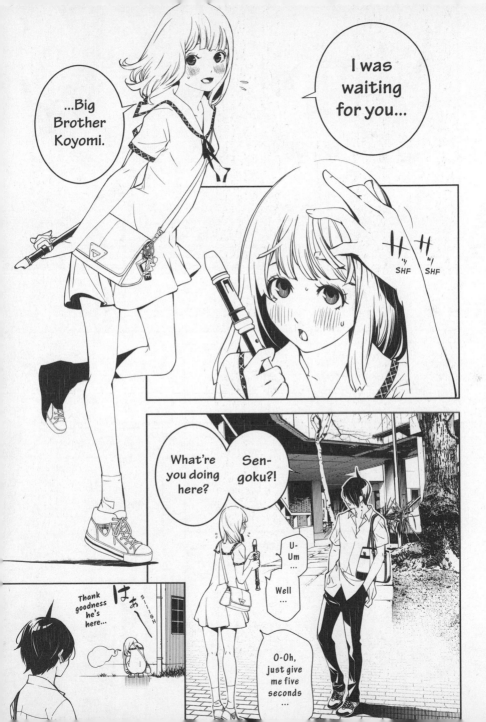

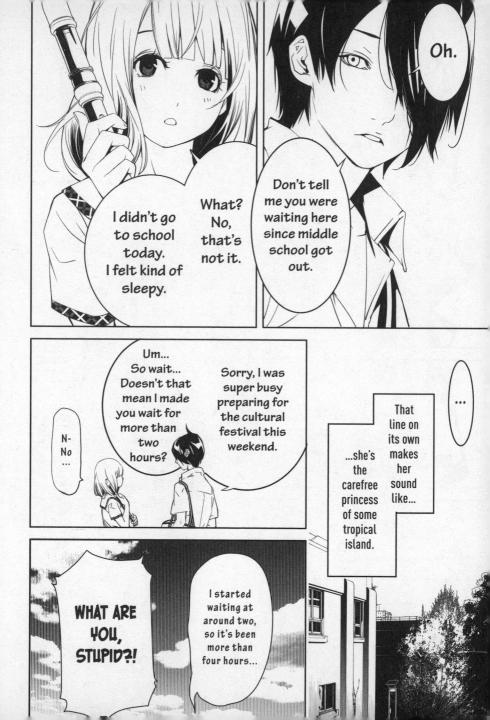

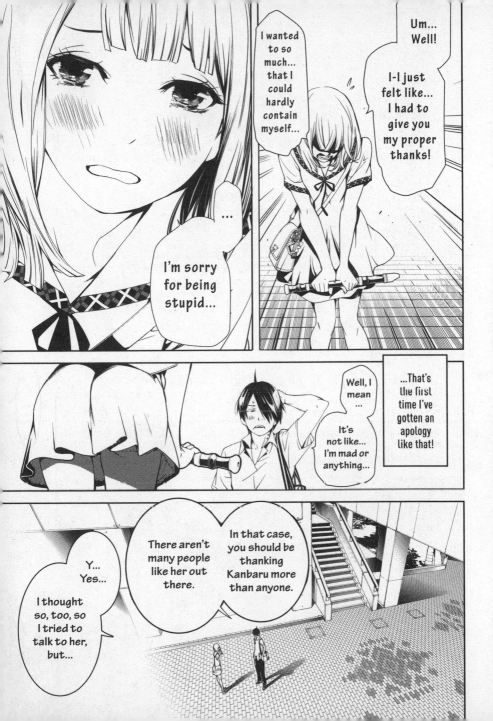

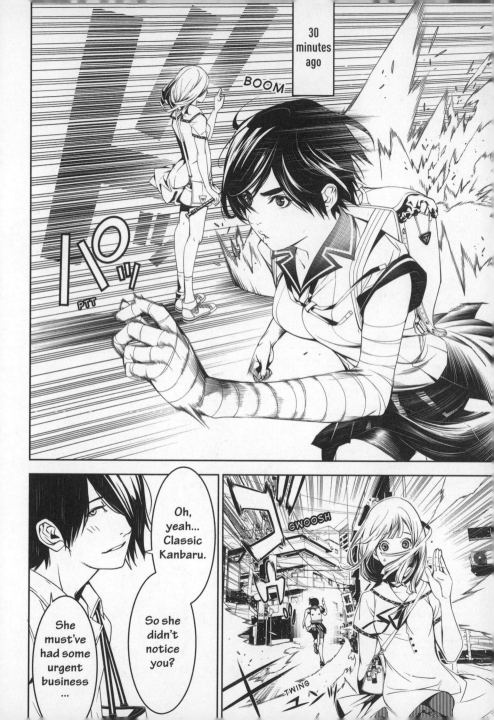

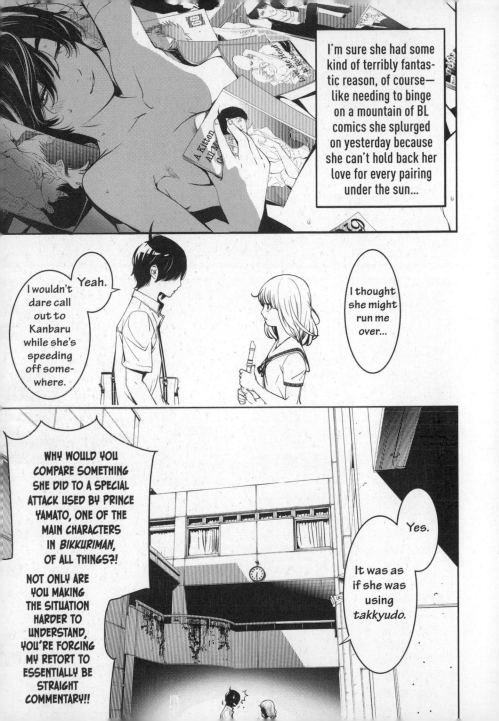

I'm sure she had some kind of terribly fantastic reason, of course— like needing to binge on a mountain of BL comics she splurged on yesterday because she can't hold back her love for every pairing under the sun...

Yeah.

I wouldn't dare call out to Kanbaru while she's speeding off some-where.

I thought she might run me over...

WHY WOULD YOU COMPARE SOMETHING SHE DID TO A SPECIAL ATTACK USED BY PRINCE YAMATO, ONE OF THE MAIN CHARACTERS IN *BIKKURIMAN*, OF ALL THINGS?!

NOT ONLY ARE YOU MAKING THE SITUATION HARDER TO UNDERSTAND, YOU'RE FORCING MY RETORT TO ESSENTIALLY BE STRAIGHT COMMENTARY!!

Yes.

It was as if she was using *takkyudo*.

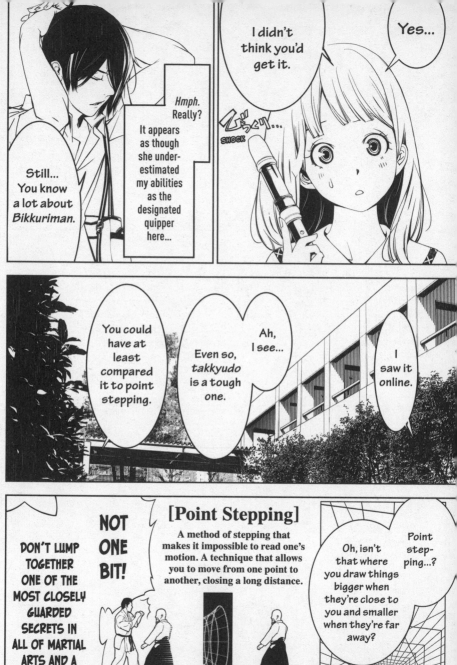

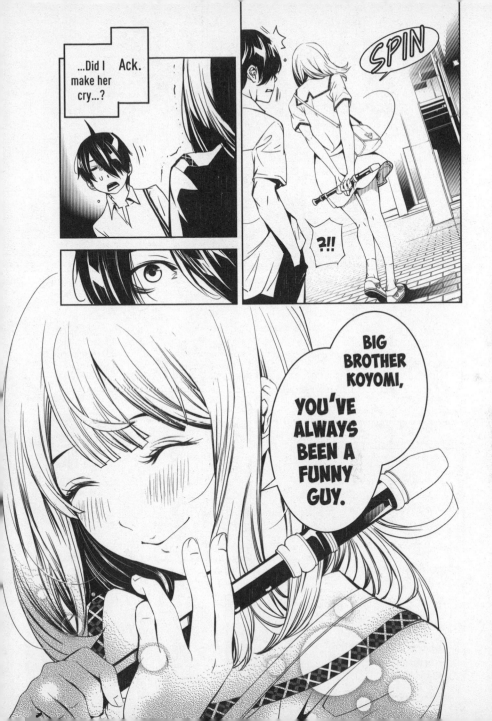

This must be your first time at a high school, right?

Oh, right.

Want to take a peek inside, then?

Is it... okay?

Hm?

Um... Yes.

...

And to blow it with all my strength if I feel like I'm in danger.

My teacher said... to never let go of it whenever I go somewhere dangerous...

Hm?

What's with that recorder?

By the way...

WHAT KIND OF TEACHER IS THAT?!

Could this teacher have been talking about a safety whistle...?

O— Oh...

AND WAIT, DO YOU REALLY FEEL LIKE YOUR LIFE IS IN DANGER JUST BECAUSE YOU'RE AT A HIGH SCHOOL?!

HOLD ON, HOLD ON! I DIDN'T EXACTLY SACRIFICE MY LIFE TO SAVE YOU! LOOK, I'M ALIVE RIGHT NOW!

So I need to value and protect my life...

You saved my life at the cost of your own...

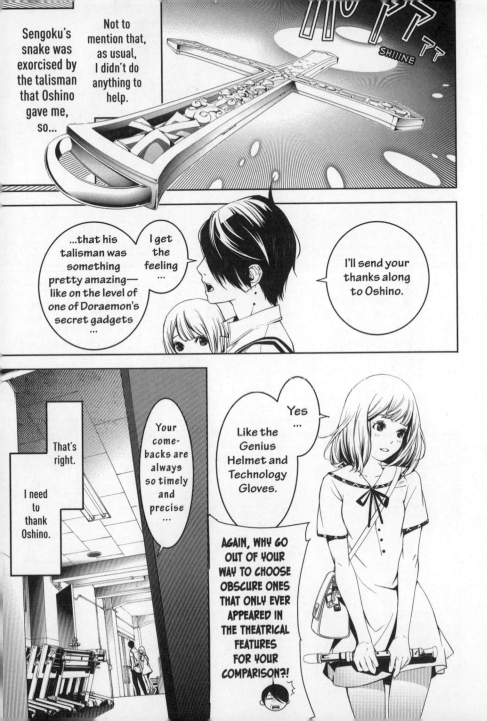

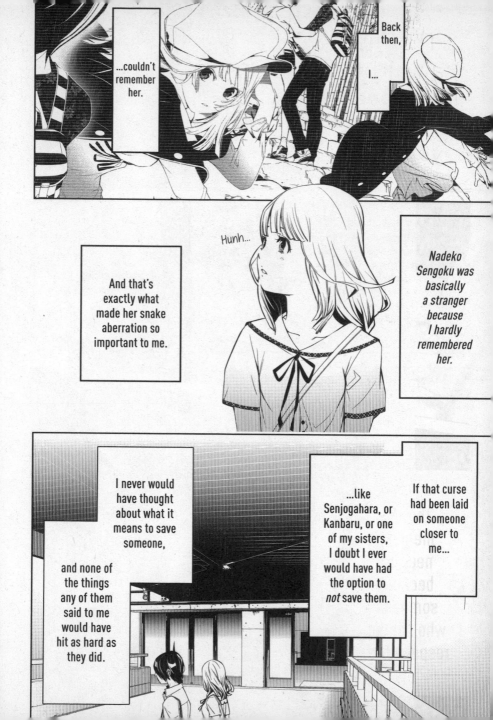

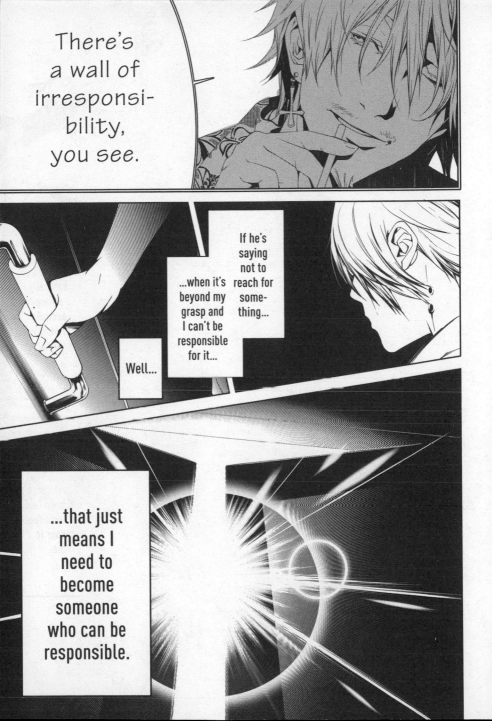

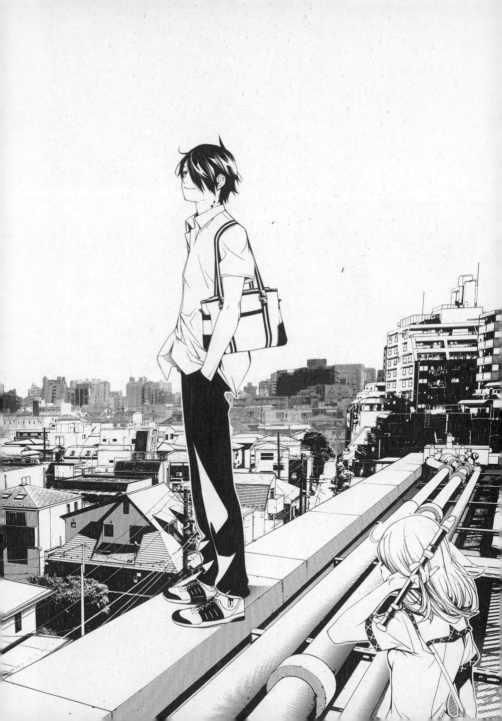

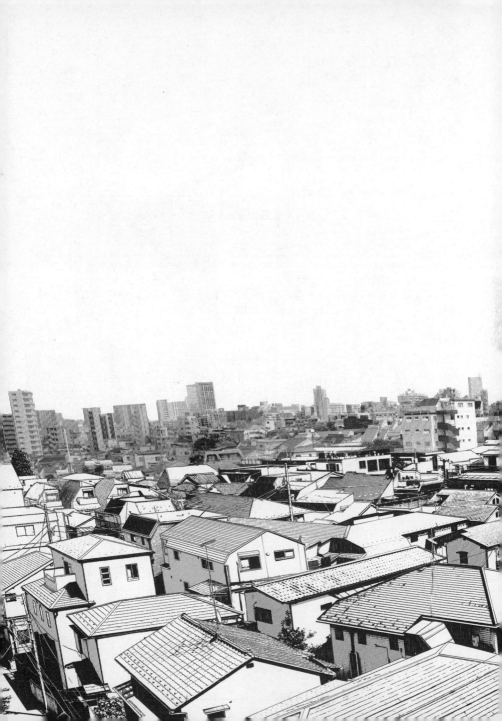

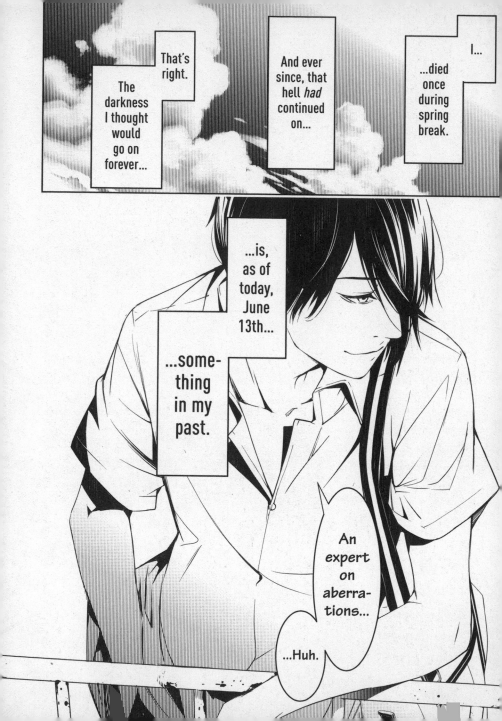

Oh.

By the way, Big Brother Koyomi...

What is it?

People say that in the movie versions of *Doraemon*, Gian suddenly becomes a weirdly grownup and good-natured character, but shouldn't they be saying that about Nobita more than anyone?

WHERE DID THAT NONSENSE QUESTION EVEN COME FROM?!

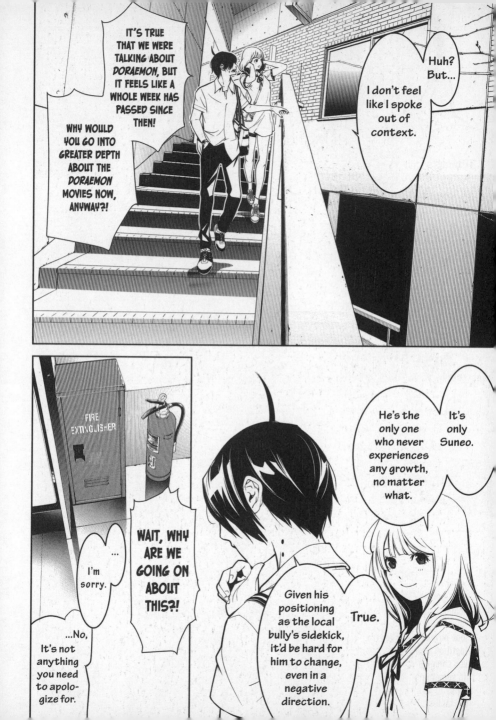

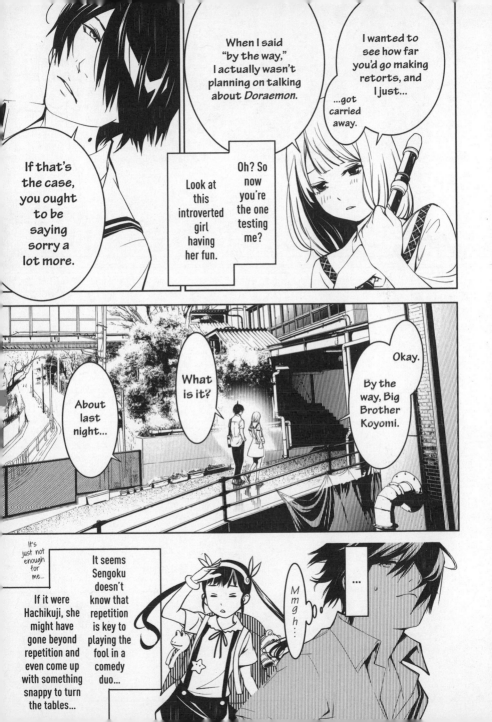

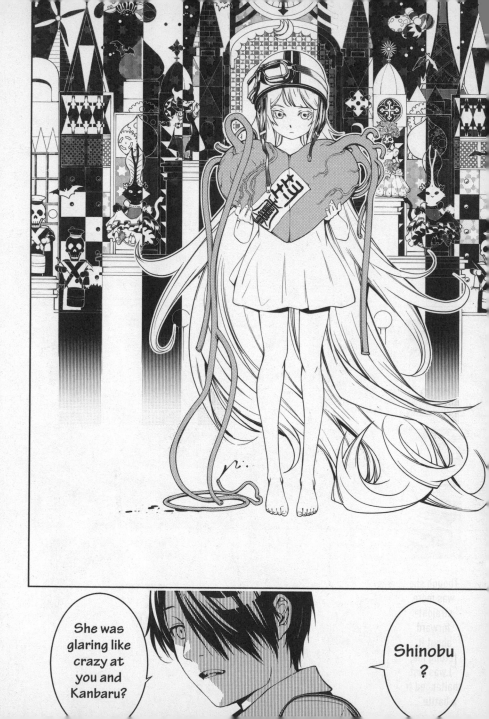

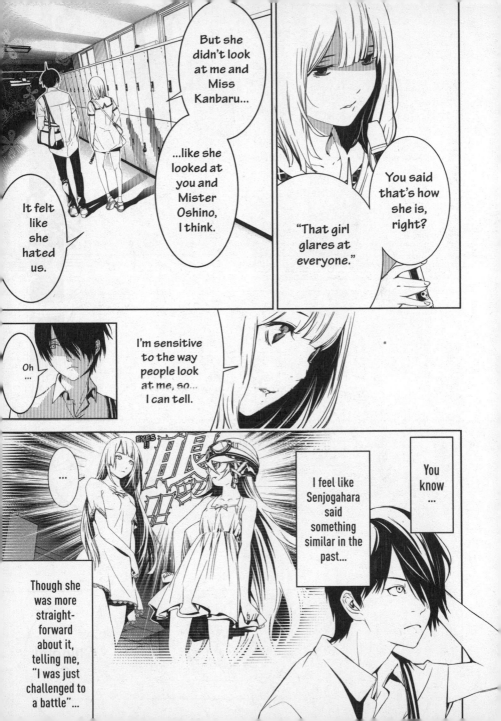

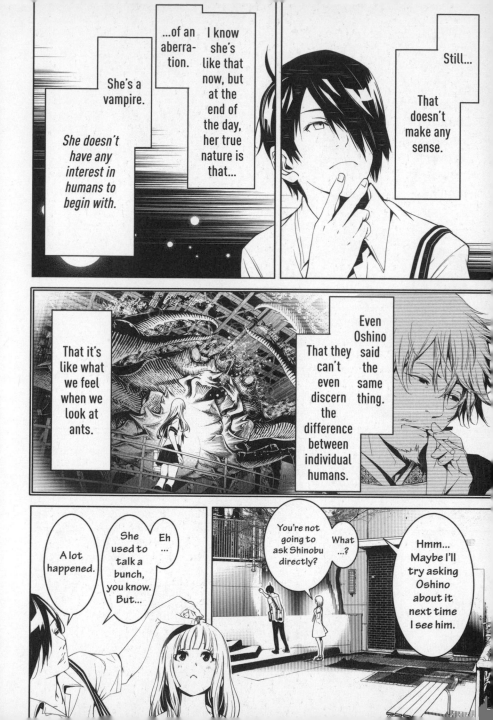

She's a vampire.

...of an aberration.

I know she's like that now, but at the end of the day, her true nature is that...

She doesn't have any interest in humans to begin with.

Still...

That doesn't make any sense.

That it's like what we feel when we look at ants.

That they can't even discern the difference between individual humans.

Even Oshino said the same thing.

A lot happened.

She used to talk a bunch, you know. But...

Eh...

You're not going to ask Shinobu directly?

What ...?

Hmm... Maybe I'll try asking Oshino about it next time I see him.

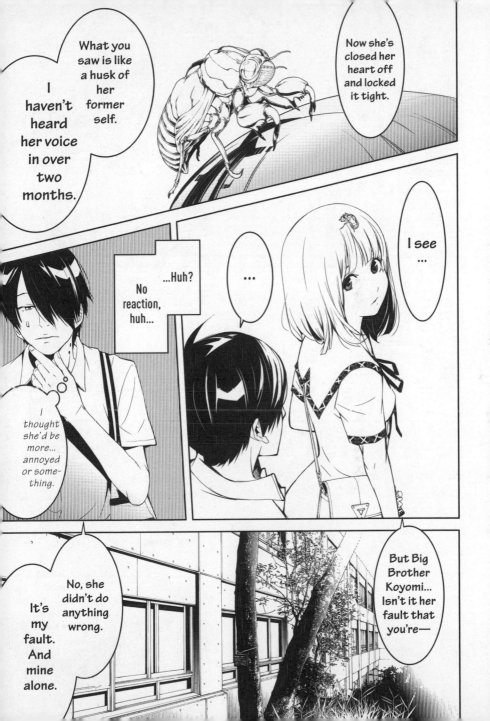

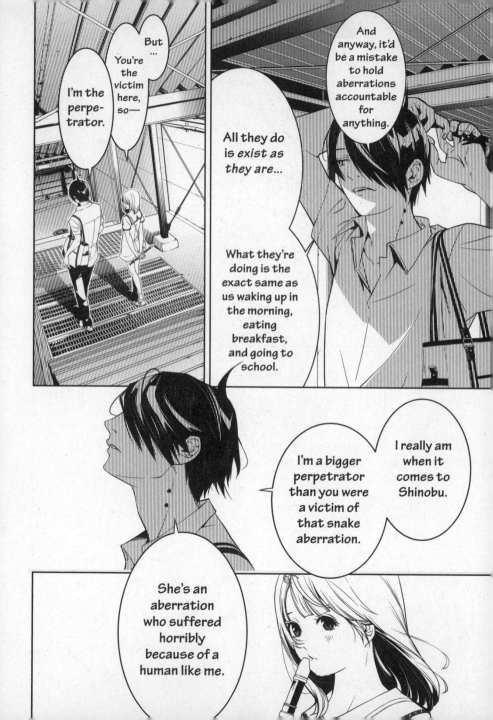

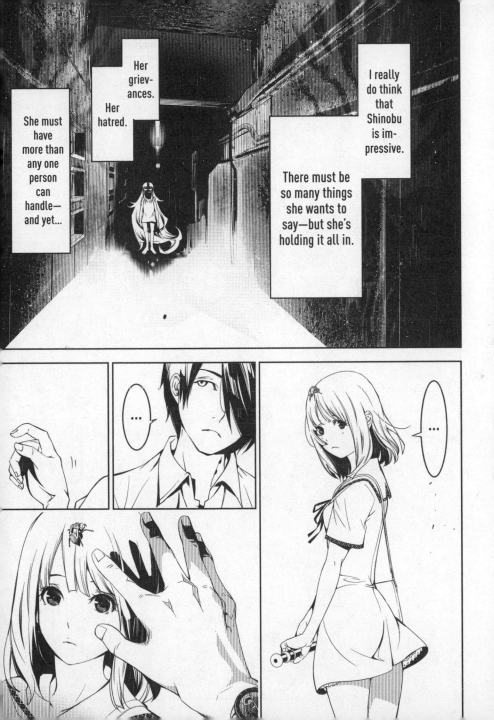

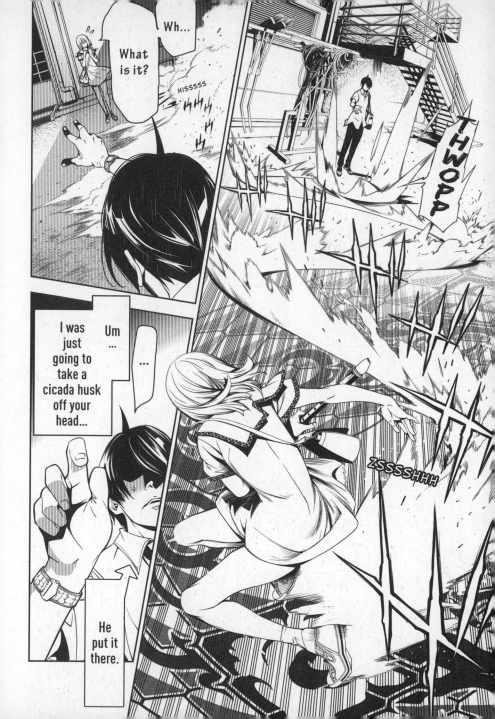

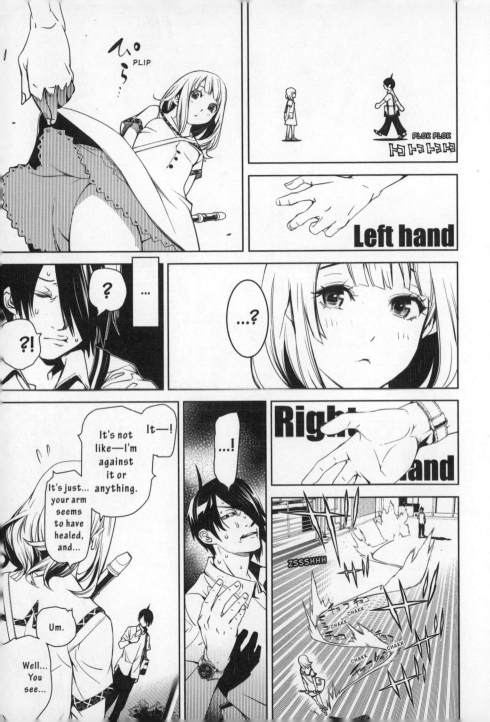

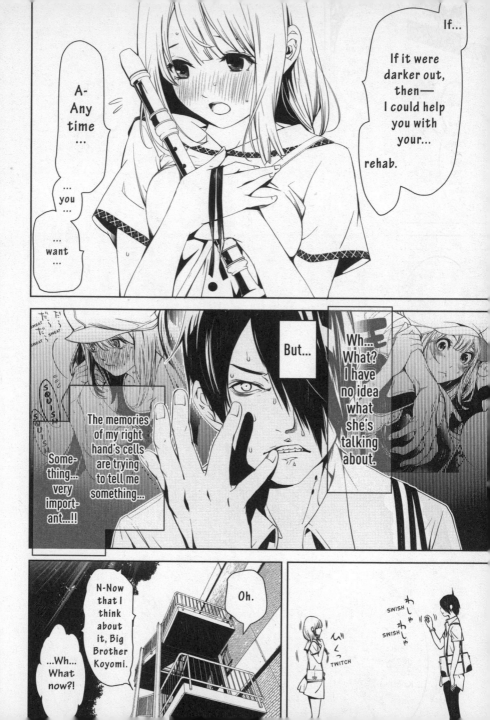

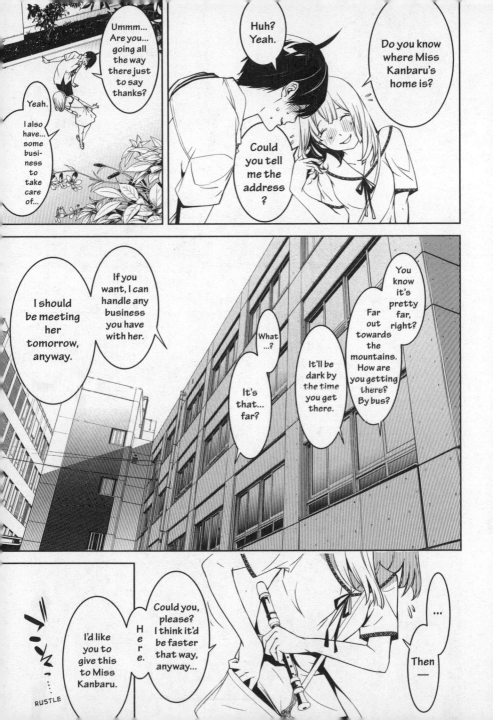

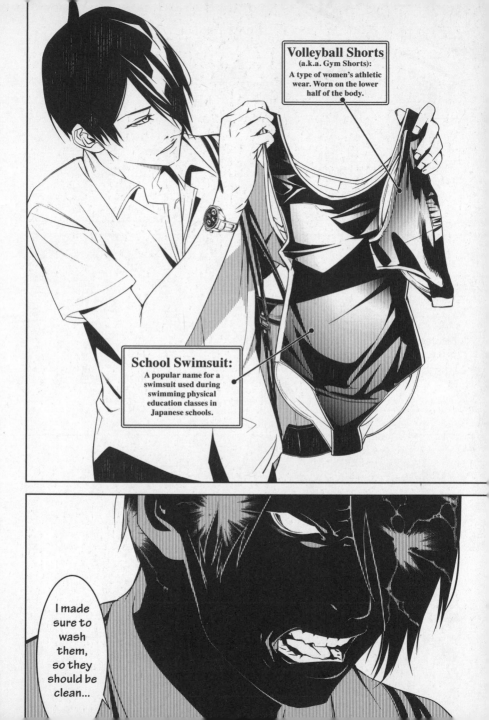

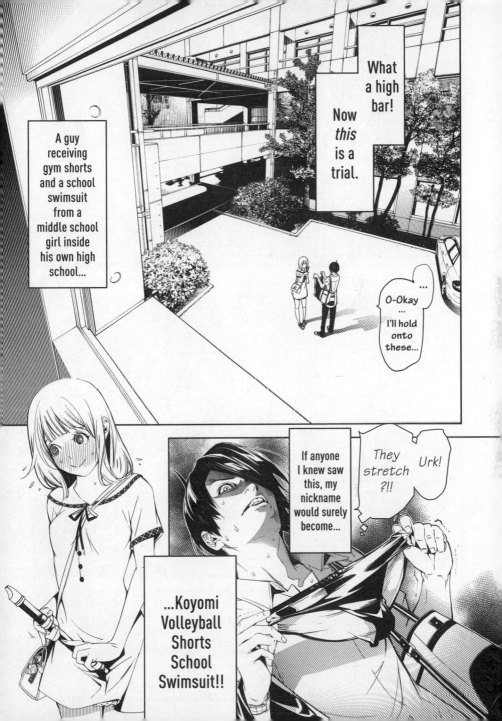

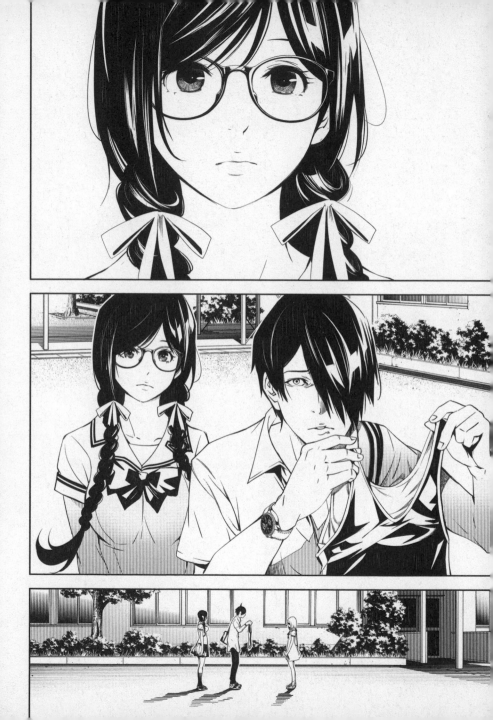

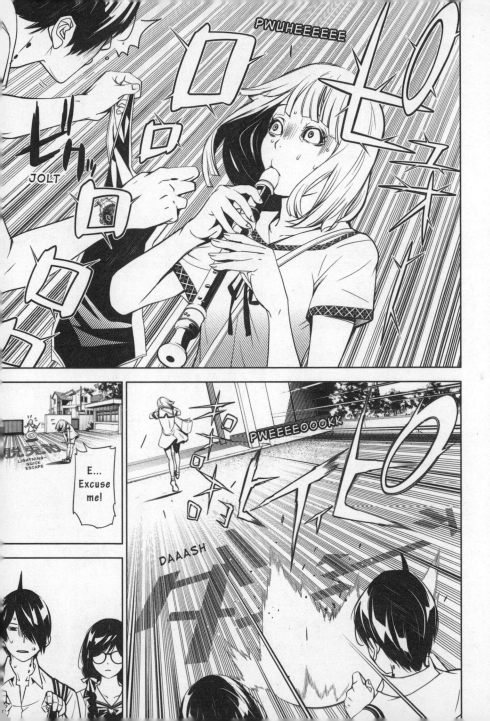

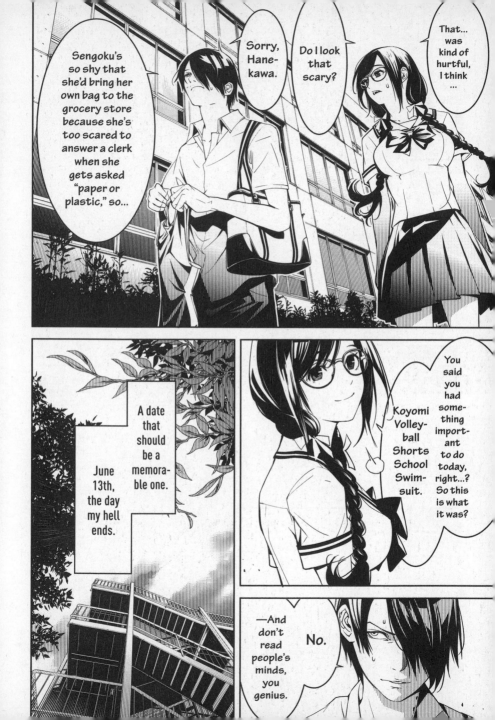

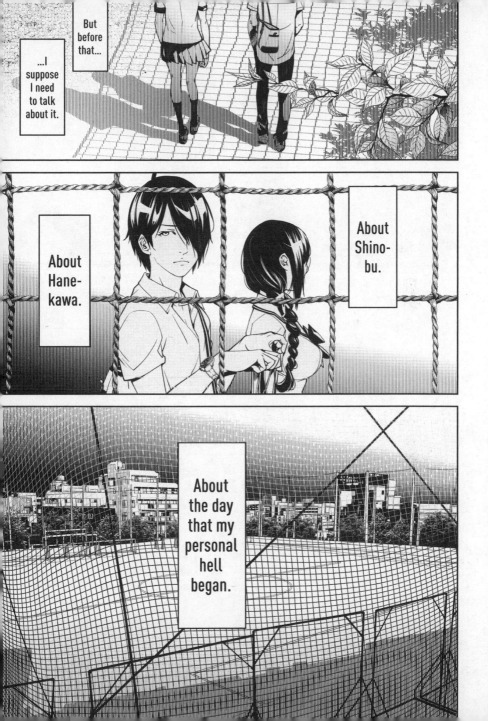

BAKEMONOGATARI

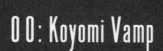

0 0: Koyomi Vamp

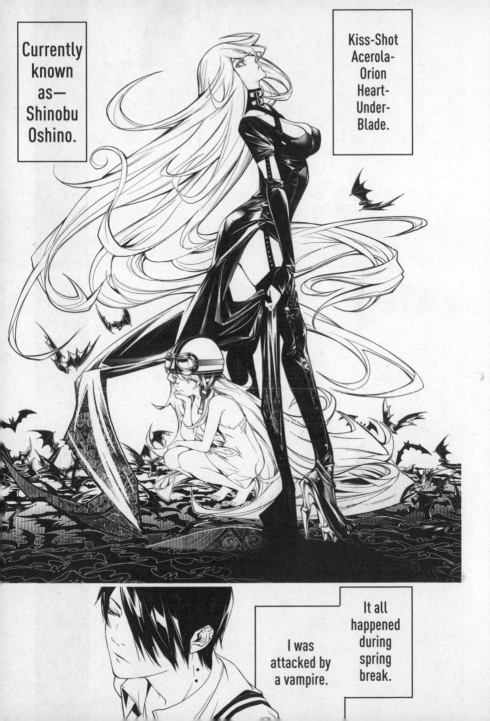

Currently known as— Shinobu Oshino.

Kiss-Shot Acerola-Orion Heart-Under-Blade.

It all happened during spring break.

I was attacked by a vampire.

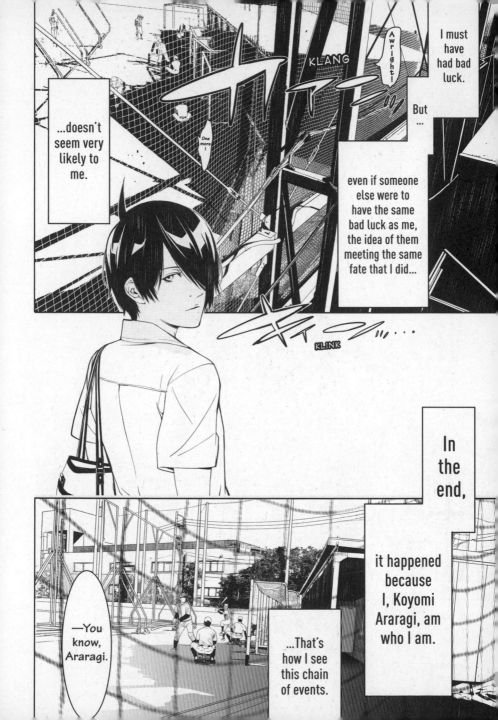

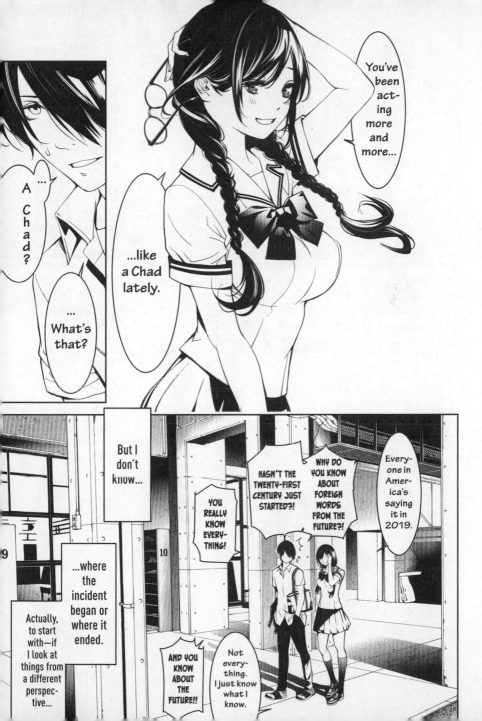

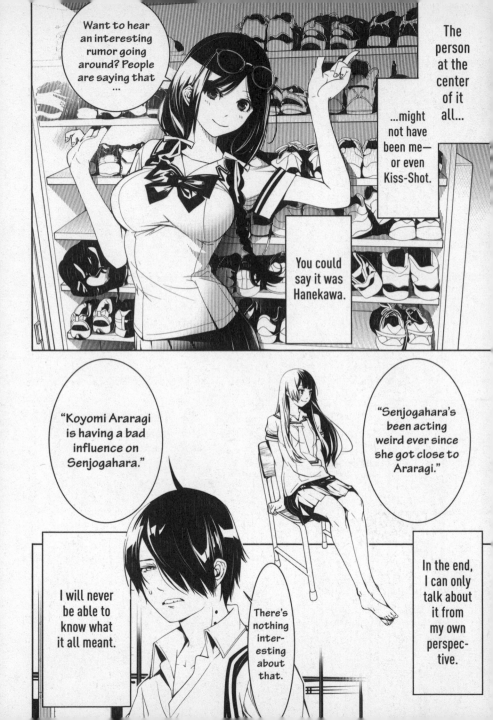

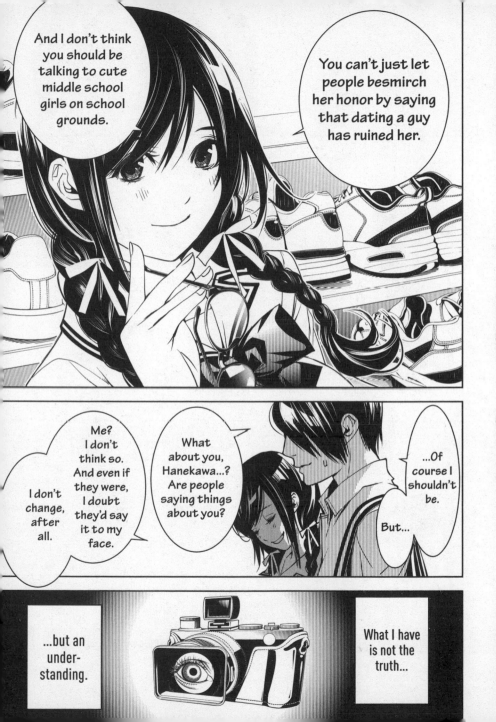

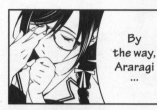

By the way, Araragi...

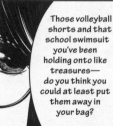

Those volleyball shorts and that school swimsuit you've been holding onto like treasures— do you think you could at least put them away in your bag?

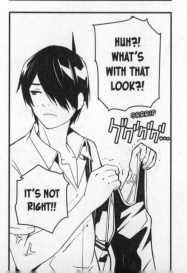

HUH?! WHAT'S WITH THAT LOOK?!

GRRRIP

IT'S NOT RIGHT!!

Something that only holds meaning for the observer. Something whose meaning changes depending on the observer. Something whose meaning cannot be agreed upon by its observers.

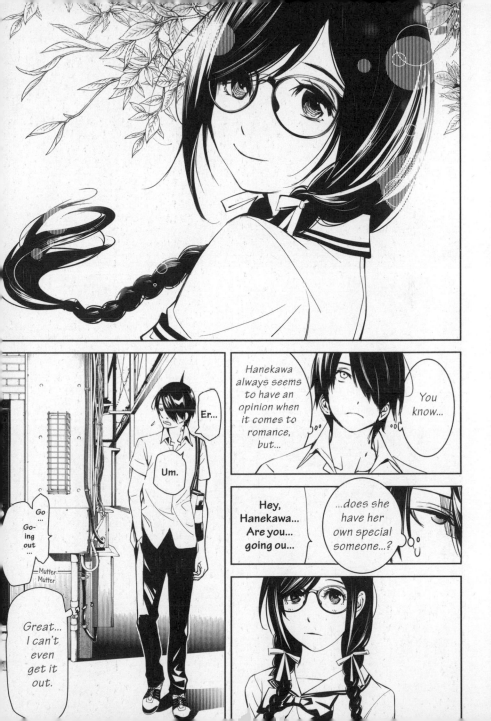

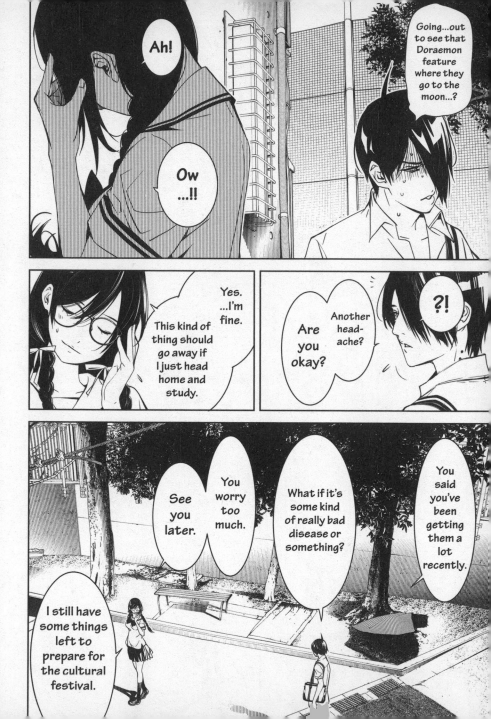

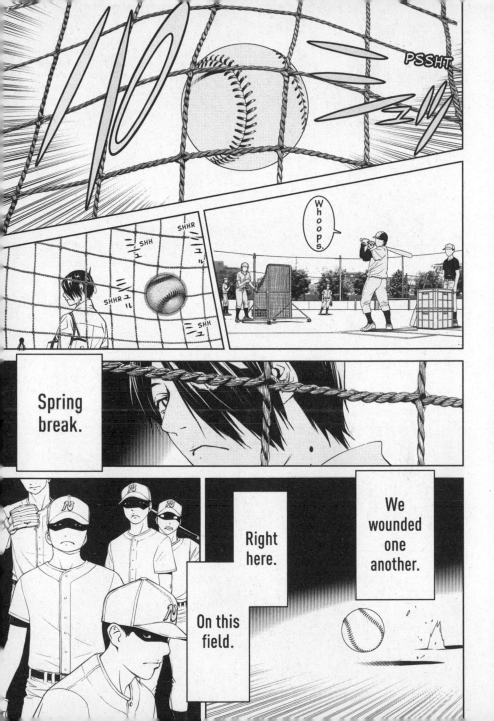

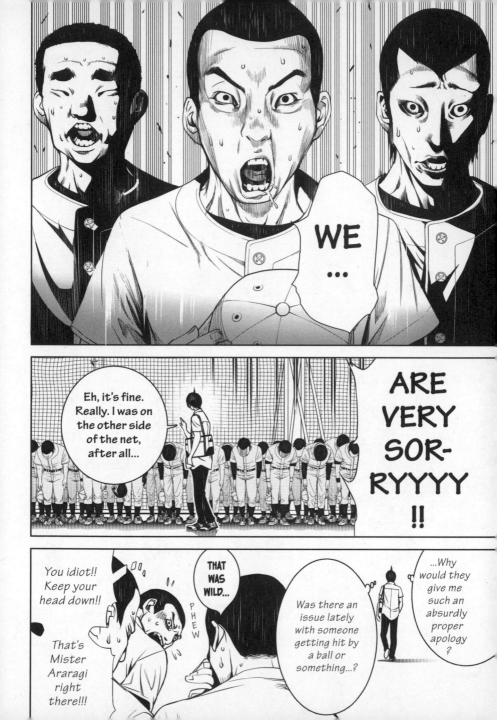

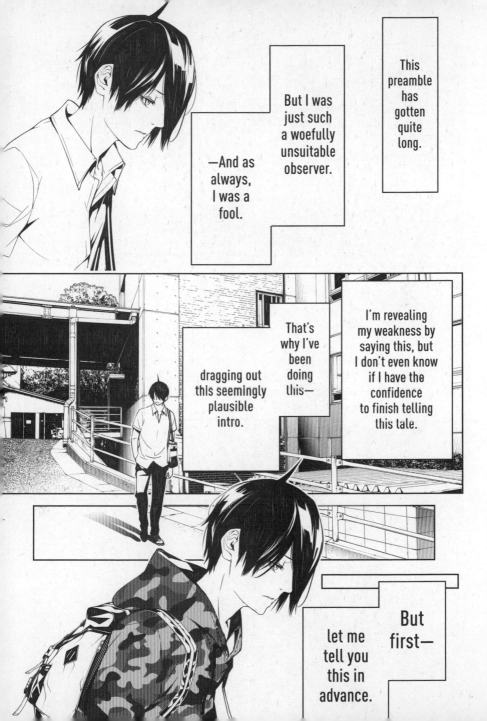

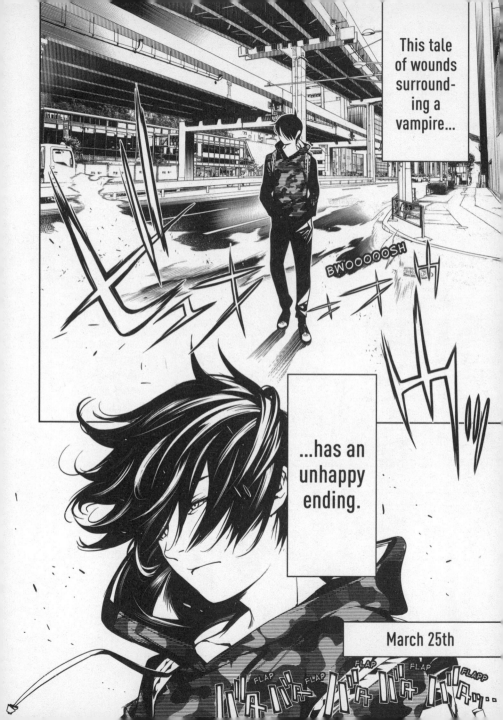

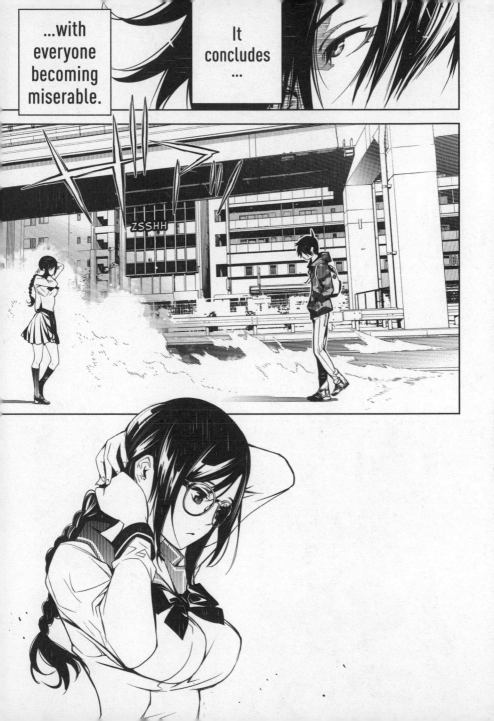

hey were ... [elegant] undergarments that refused to
[r]elease one's gaze once a pair of eyes was attracted
[t]o them. They were a tidy and pure whit[e]
was not as if they were suggestively shaped
[f]act, they seemed to be on the high
[...]end of the surface area s[...]
[...]rum. A wide article, made of th[...]
[...]cloth—by no means la[...]
[...]civious, and in fact, if one
[...]were to speak of them in that
[...]way, it would be reasonabl[...]
[...]o call them demure [...]
[...]hey were ... white it[...]
[...]zzli[...]

[...] the
[...] white stri[ng]
[...]en used to
[...]icate e[...]
[...]ered pattern[...]
[...]hite canva[s]
[...] doubt intended to [...]
[...] flowers. The pat[...]
[...]ern, with its bilater[al]
[...]ymmetry, acted t[...]
[...]ring a sublime balanc[e]
[...]o the piece as a whole
[...]nd toward the top-cente[r]
[...]f the embroidery sa[...]
[...]all ribbon. This one
[...]orked to further c[...]

What's more, visibl[e] above that sm[all] ribbon was h[er] abdomen an[d] cute belly butt[on]. Yes, her skirt had b[een] flipped so far up tha[t] those parts of her were now immodestly exposed. Had I wan[ted] I could even have [recog]nized the tails of [?] tucked into her [?]

[?]ver [?]new t[?] [?]he shirt[?] [?]f a blouse [?] [?]ning of a [?] [?] my eyes. [?]irts, they [?] [?]us exis- [?]

could appear so sala[ci]ous. T[he?] [?]irt was another fresh sight [?] [?]le I frequently caught sight o[f] [?]ed to be inviolable, myste- [?]s—but I now felt as though, for [?] [?]tood the structure of this [?]

[?]t of all, i[t?] only the front sec[tion] [?] her skirt was flipped. Next [to?] [?]er pure-white undergarme[nt?] stood something else so proudly white it was as if the two were in competition: her thighs, which had no small amount of meat o[n] [t]hem. Sitting behind the two, h[er?] [na]vy-blue skirt placed the[m?]

ame across

de of fine

upled with th

oined behind

ed as if she was

d underwear

ppeared

This was it.

The moment of first contact between me and Tsubasa Hanekawa.

could say her skir... longer tha... the averag girl's, was serving like a blackou... centuate a graceful... en the skirt's ... like they migh... velvet. And w... pose of hers, her ... her head, it practicall... off her v... was...

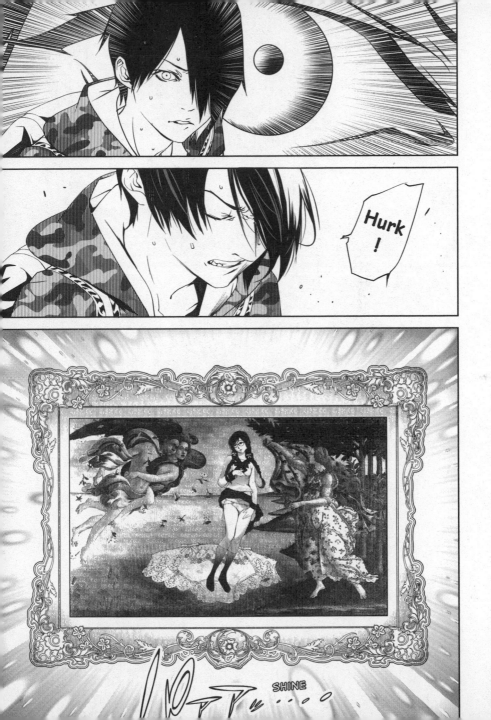

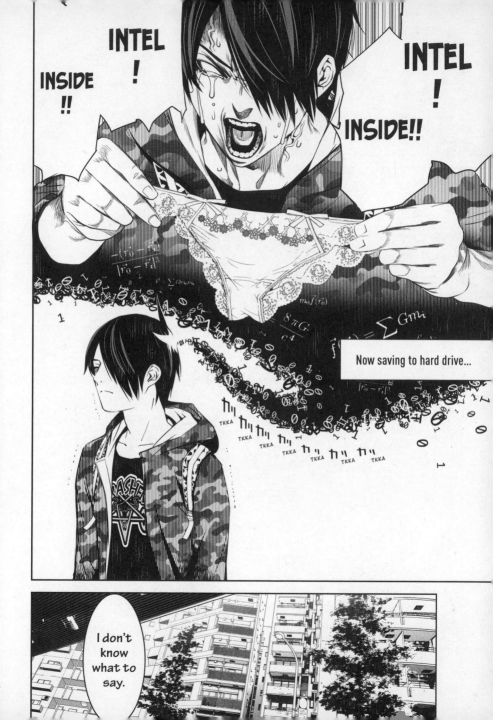

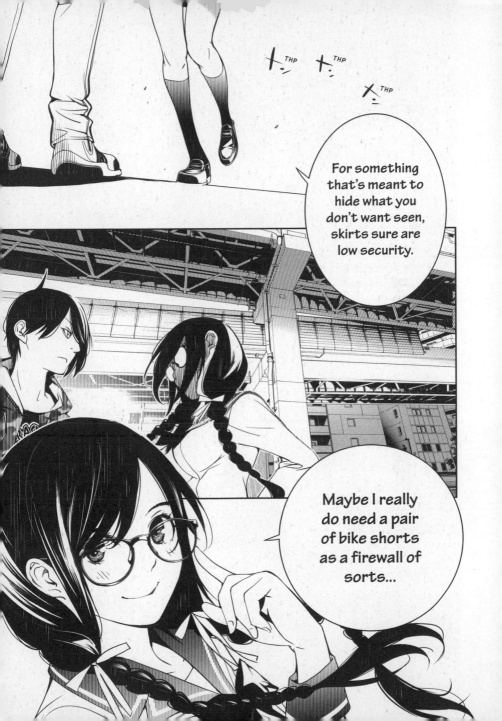

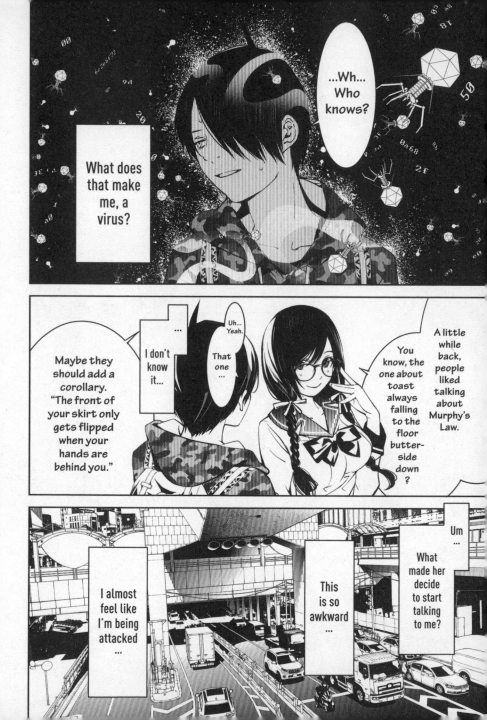

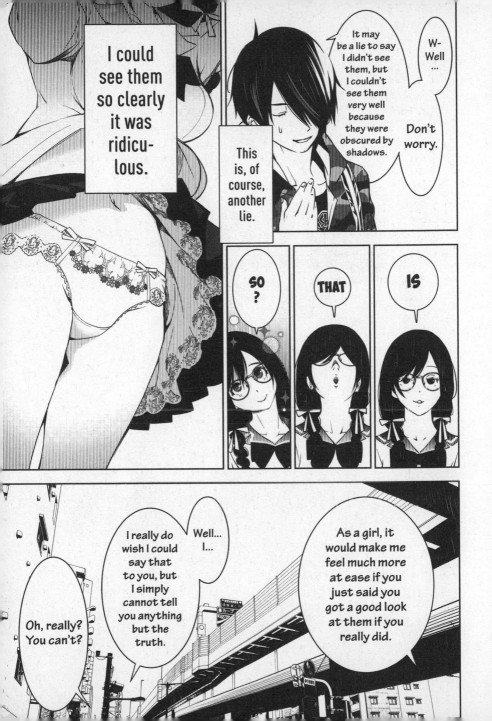

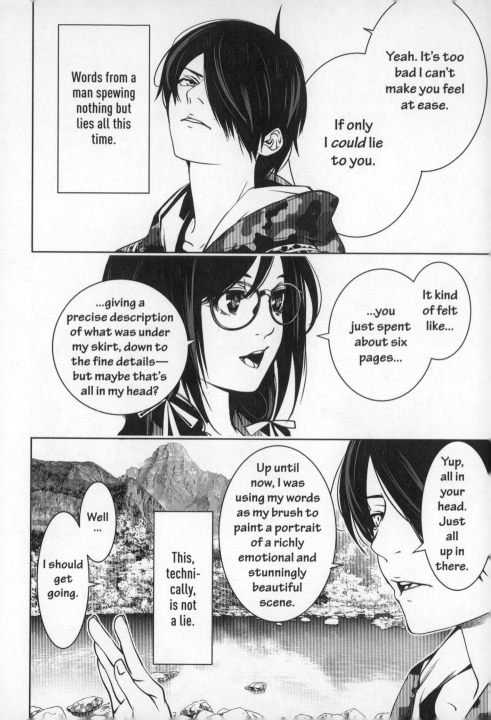

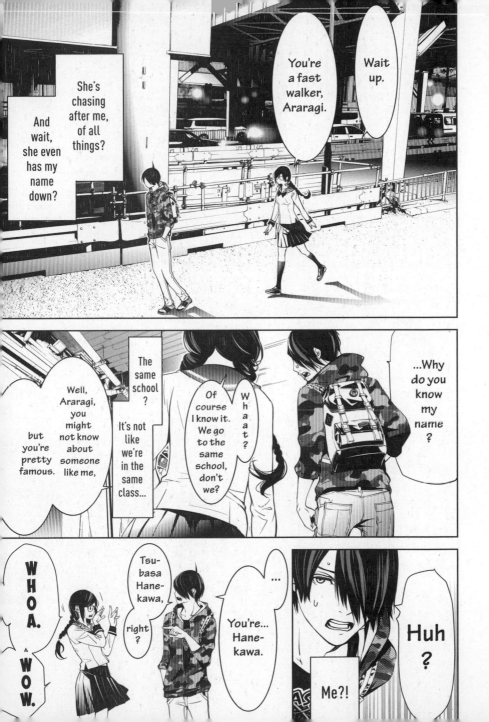

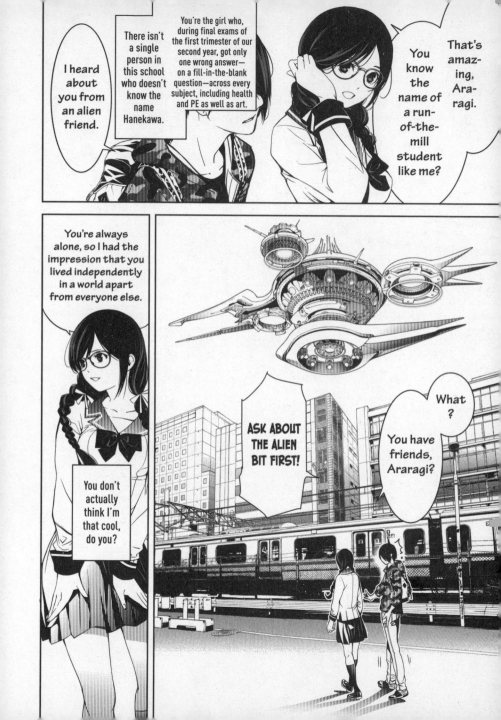

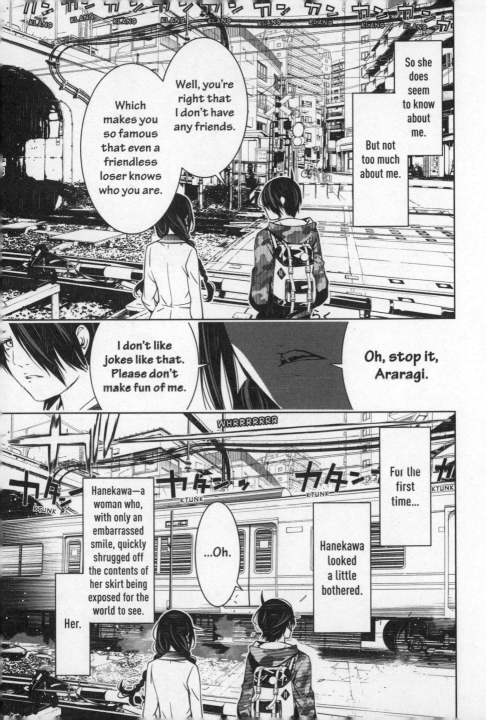

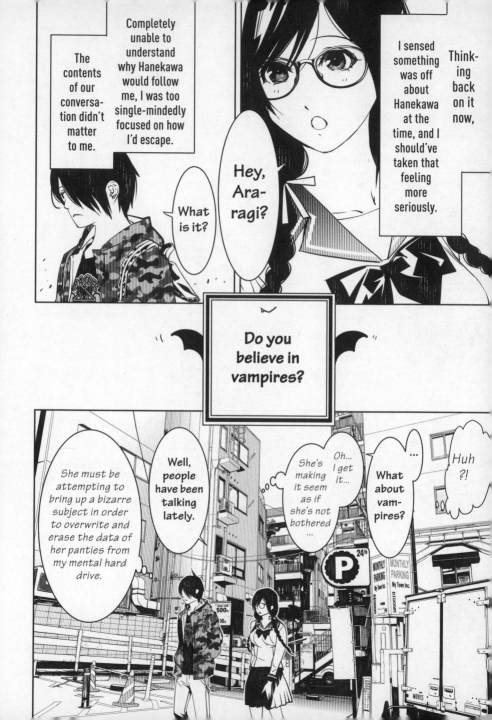

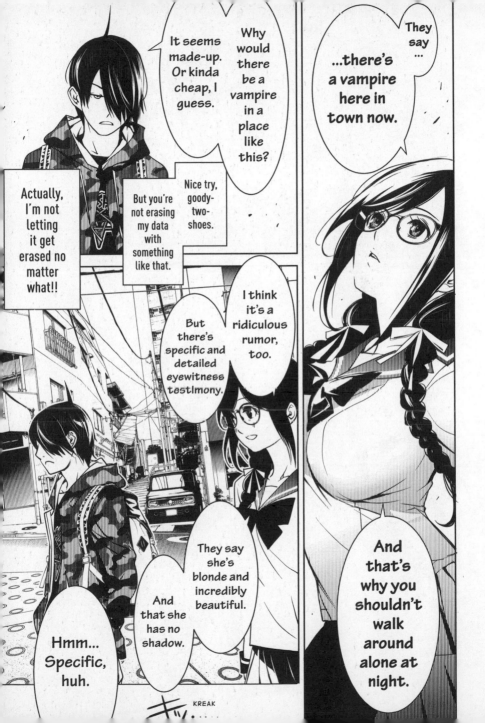

It seems made-up. Or kinda cheap, I guess.

Why would there be a vampire in a place like this?

They say...

...there's a vampire here in town now.

Actually, I'm not letting it get erased no matter what!!

But you're not erasing my data with something like that.

Nice try, goody-two-shoes.

But there's specific and detailed eyewitness testImony.

I think it's a ridiculous rumor, too.

And that's why you shouldn't walk around alone at night.

They say she's blonde and incredibly beautiful.

And that she has no shadow.

Hmm... Specific, huh.

KREAK

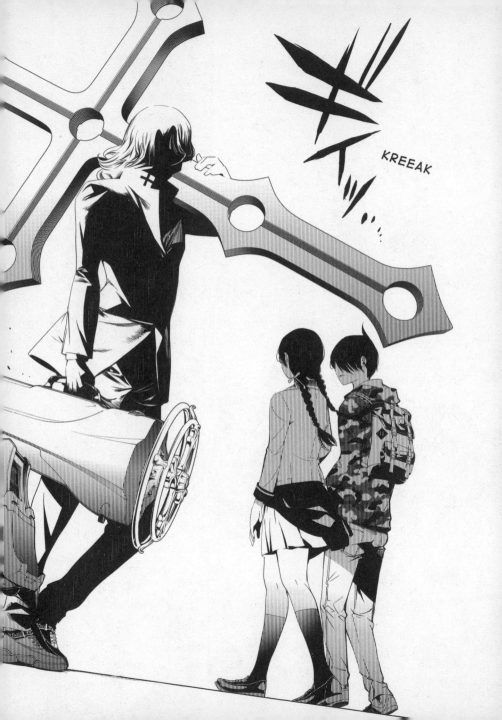

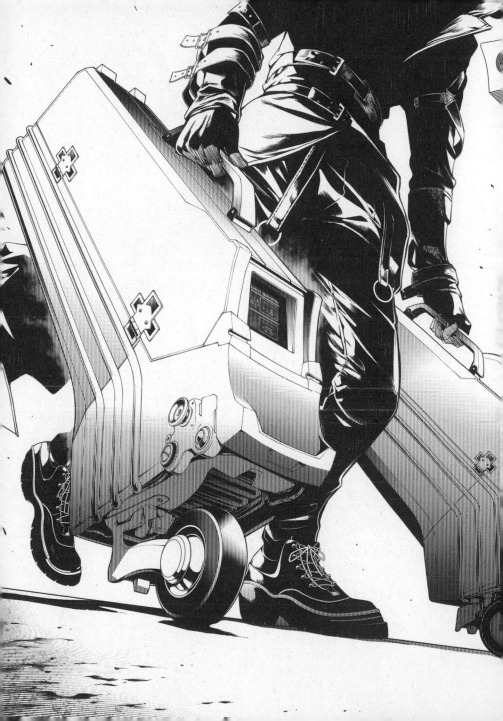

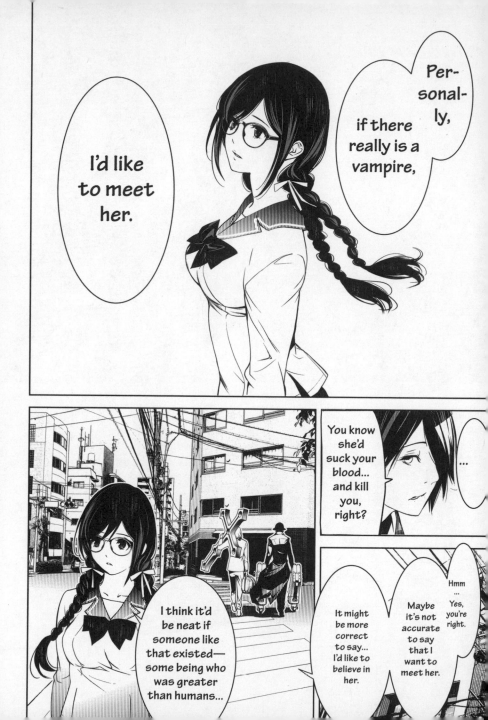

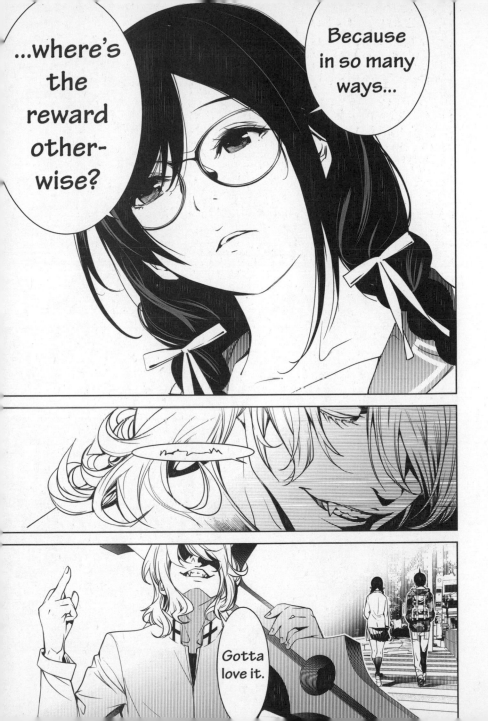

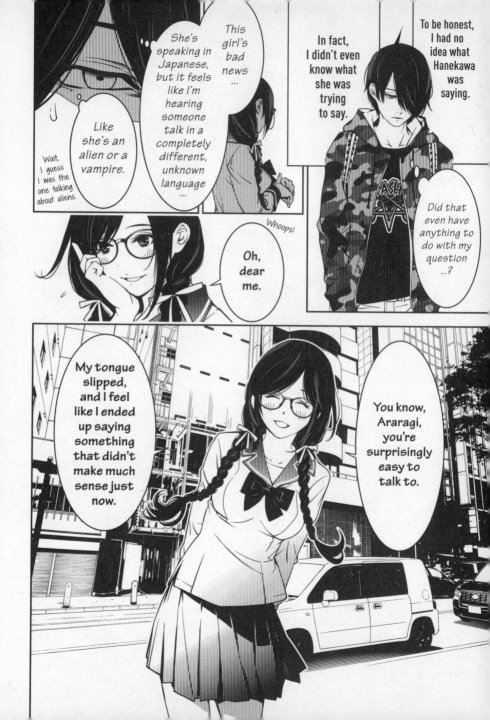

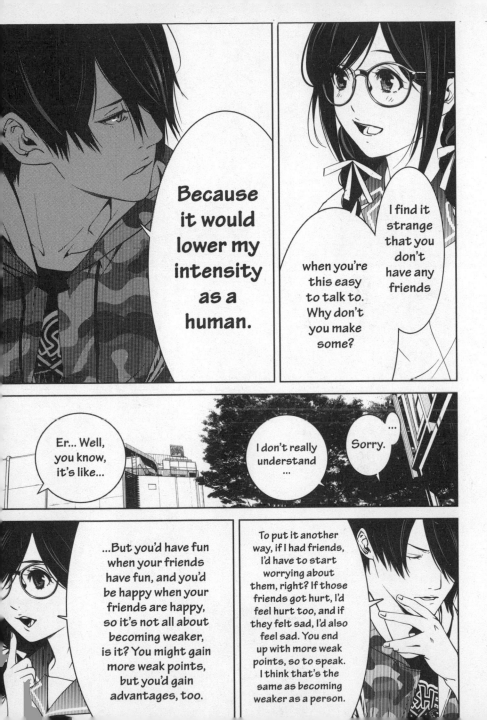

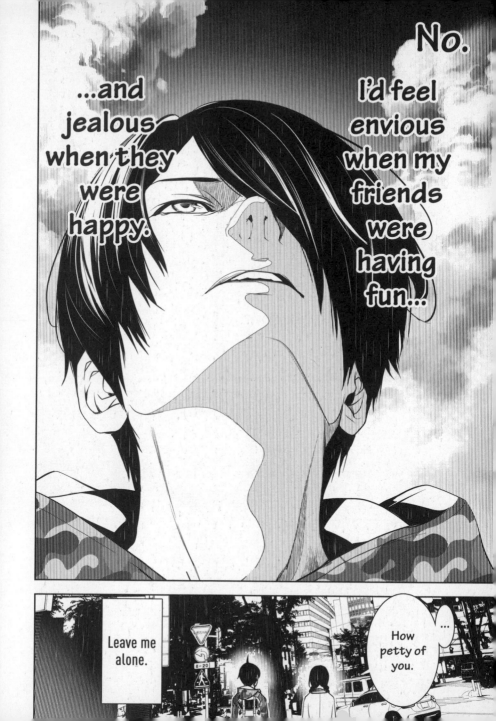

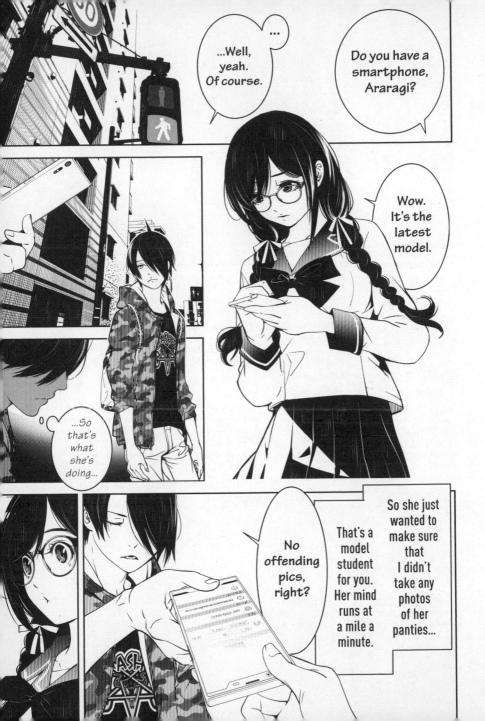

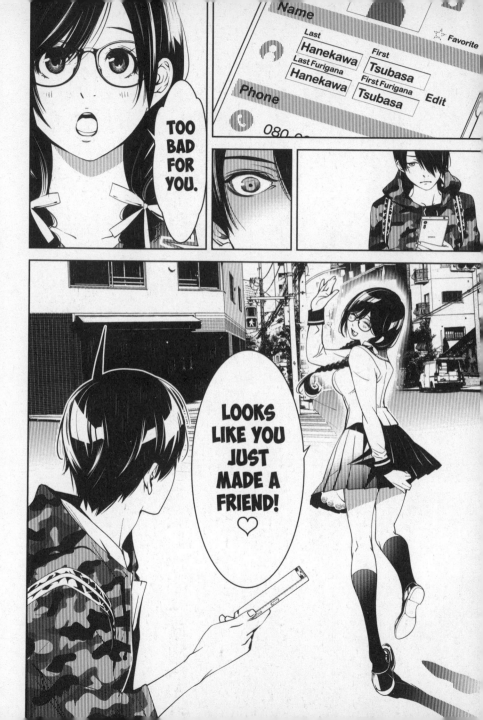

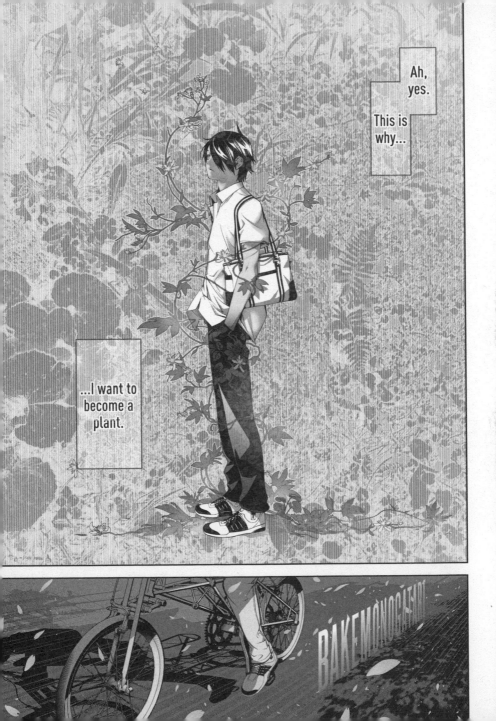

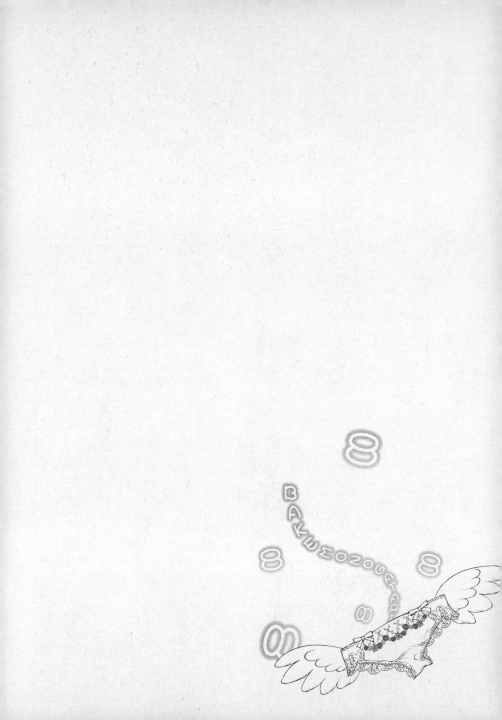

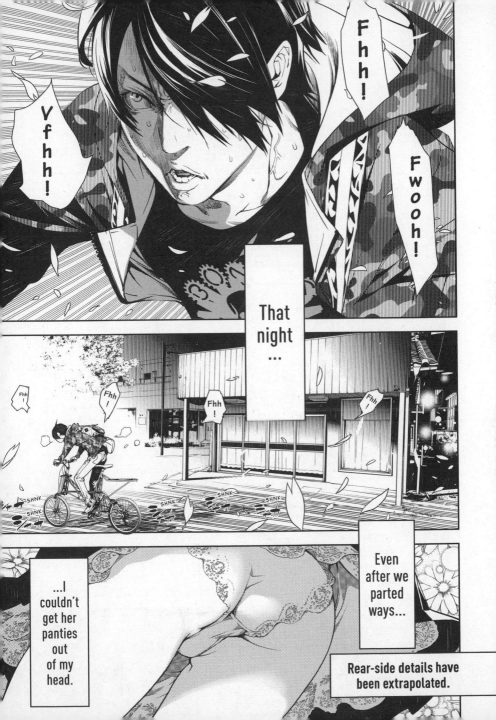

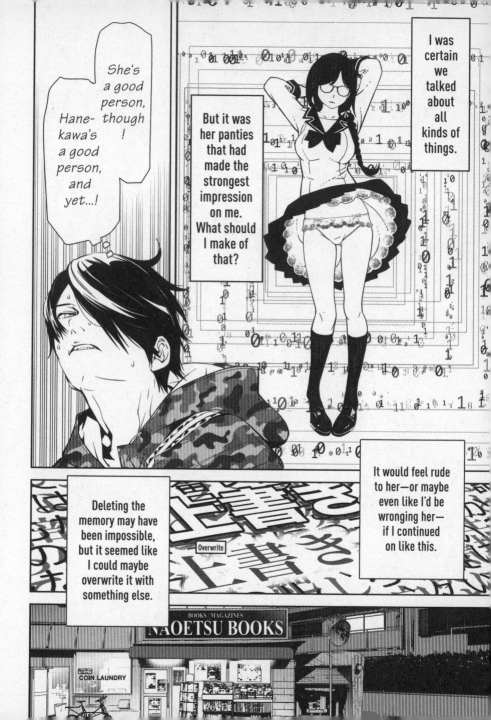

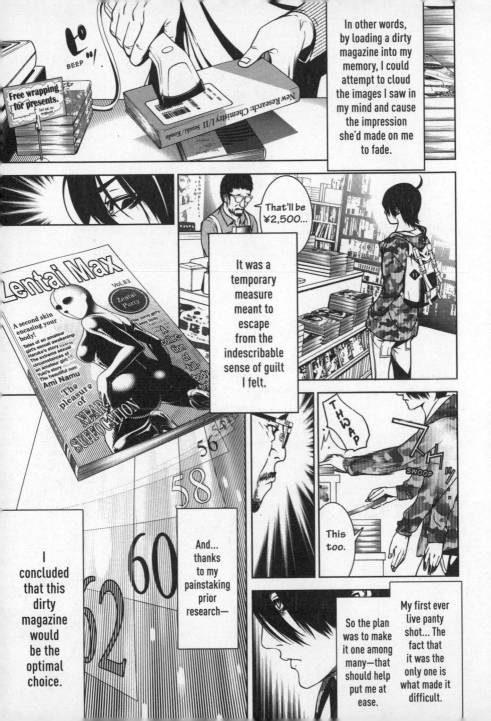

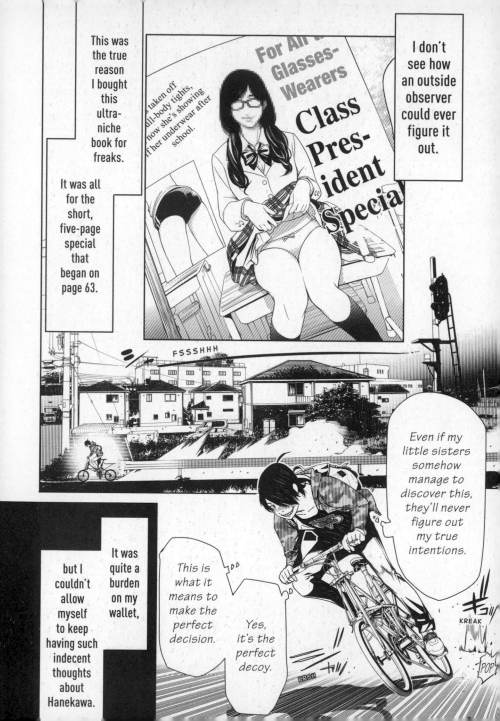

This was the true reason I bought this ultra-niche book for freaks.

It was all for the short, five-page special that began on page 63.

For All Glasses-Wearers

...s taken off ...all-body tights, ...how she's showing ...f her underwear after school.

Class Pres- ident Special

I don't see how an outside observer could ever figure it out.

FSSSHHH

Even if my little sisters somehow manage to discover this, they'll never figure out my true intentions.

but I couldn't allow myself to keep having such indecent thoughts about Hanekawa.

It was quite a burden on my wallet,

This is what it means to make the perfect decision.

Yes, it's the perfect decoy.

KREAK

POP

KRSH

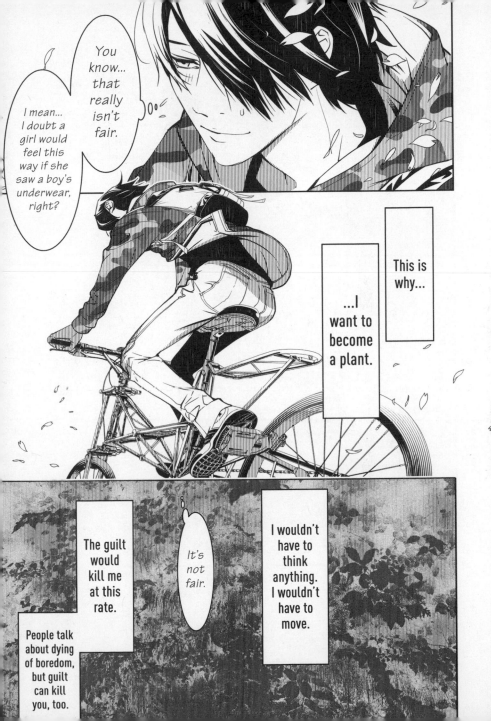

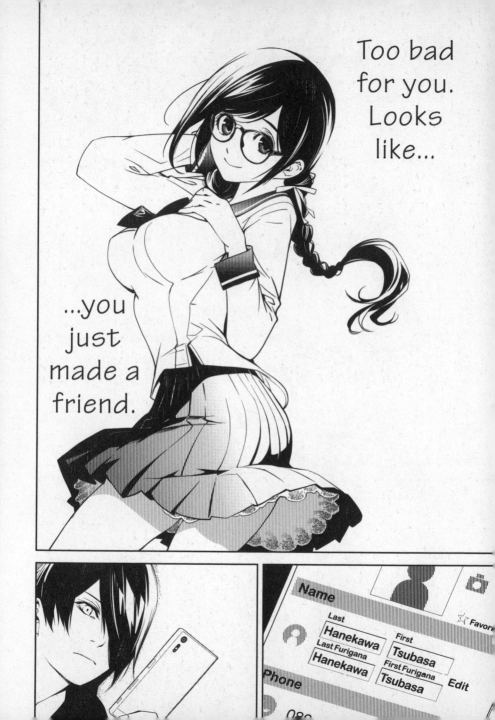

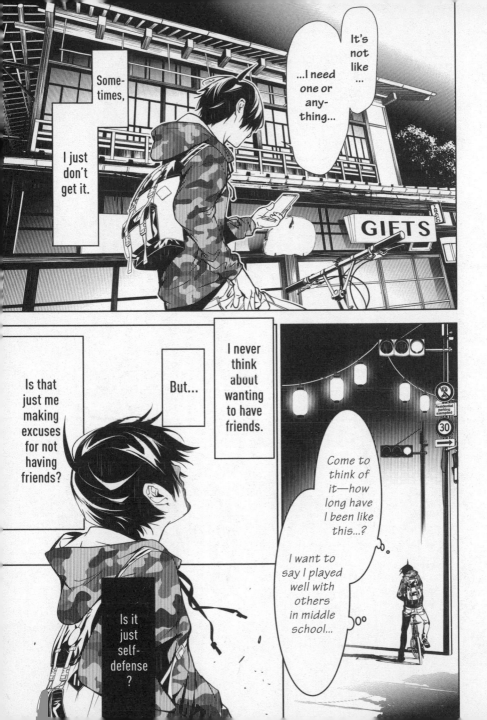

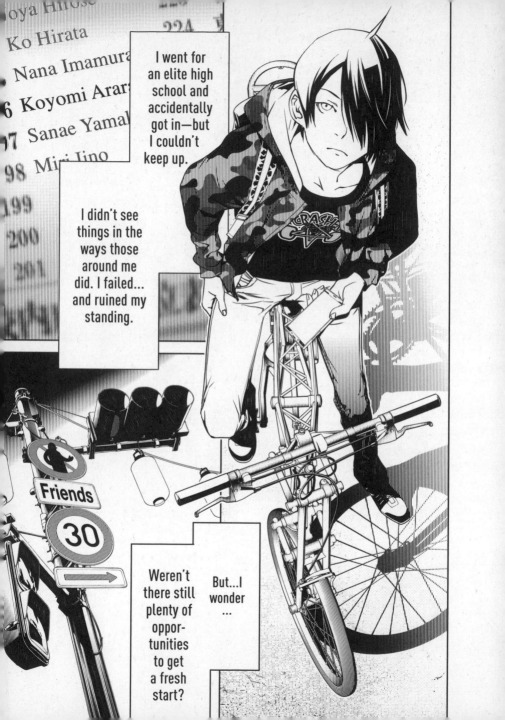

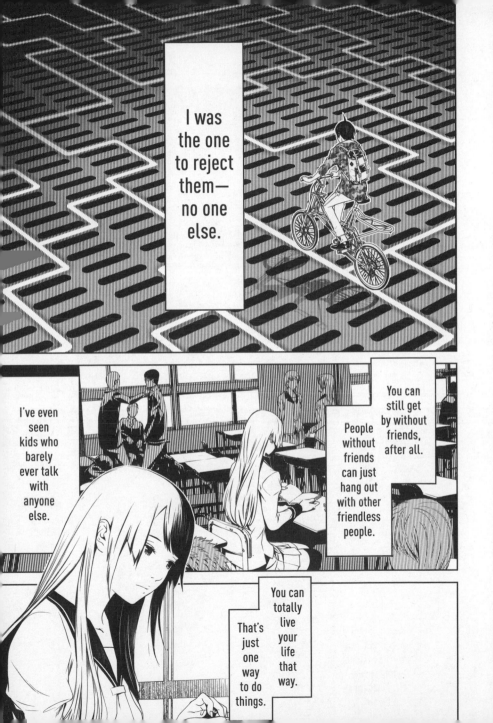

I was the one to reject them—no one else.

I've even seen kids who barely ever talk with anyone else.

People without friends can just hang out with other friendless people.

You can still get by without friends, after all.

That's just one way to do things.

You can totally live your life that way.

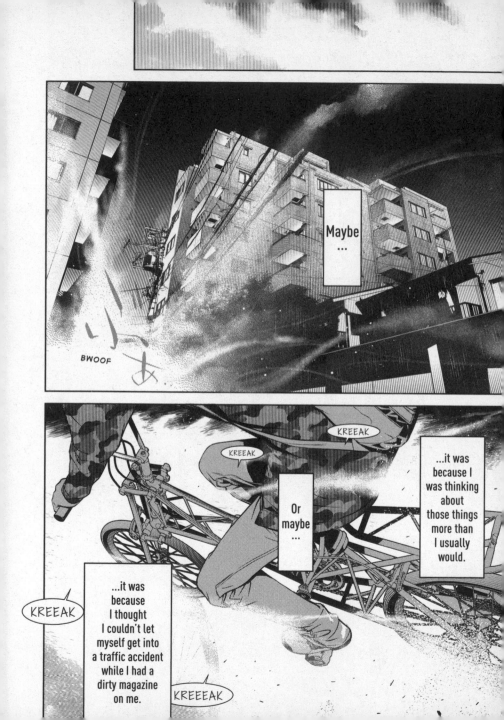

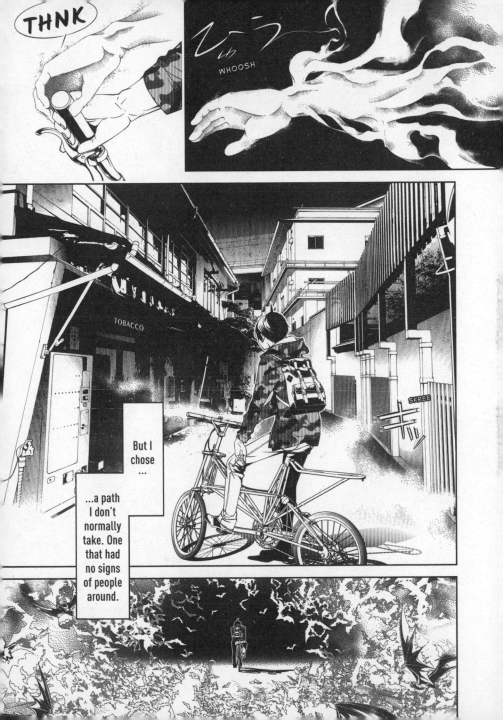

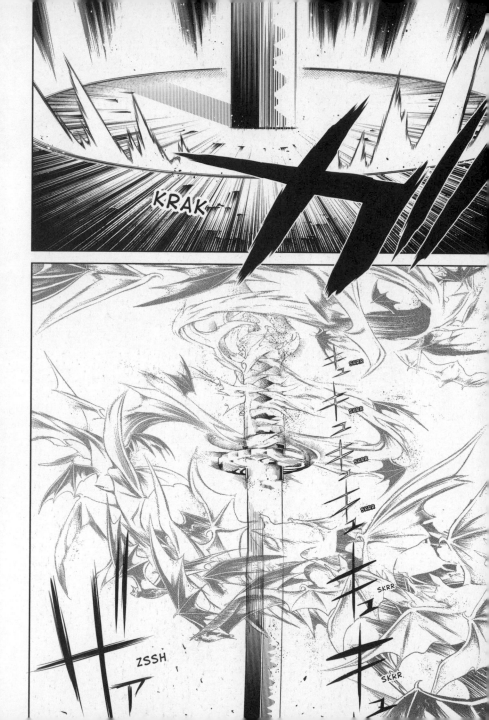

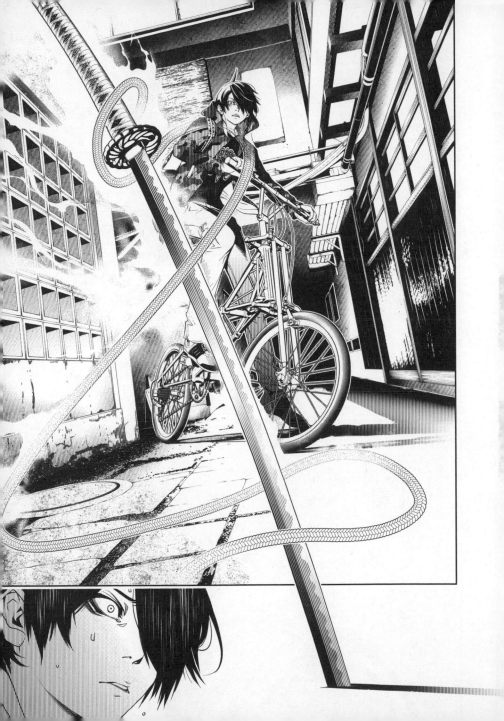

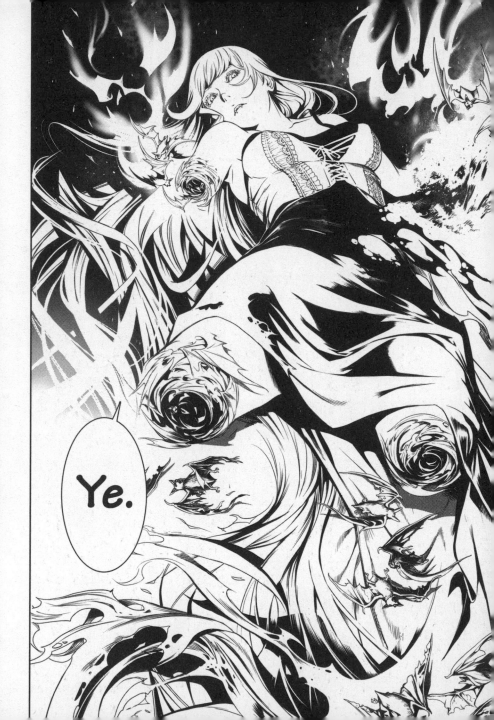

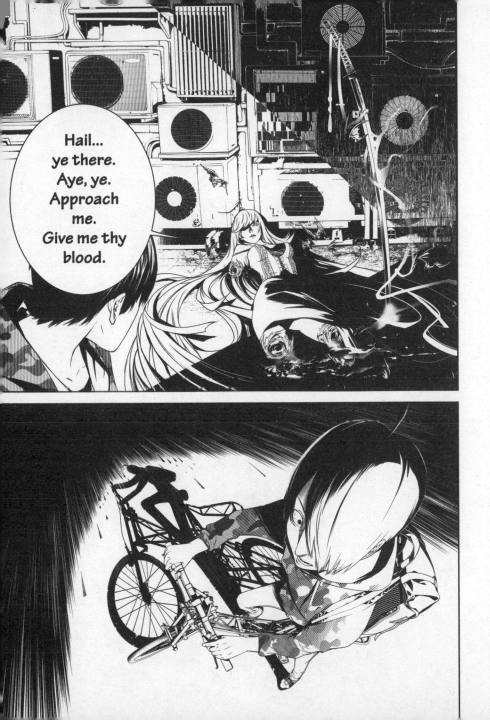

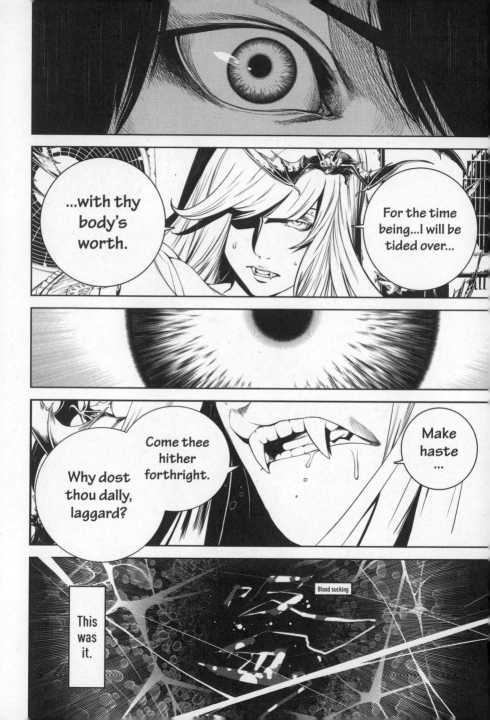

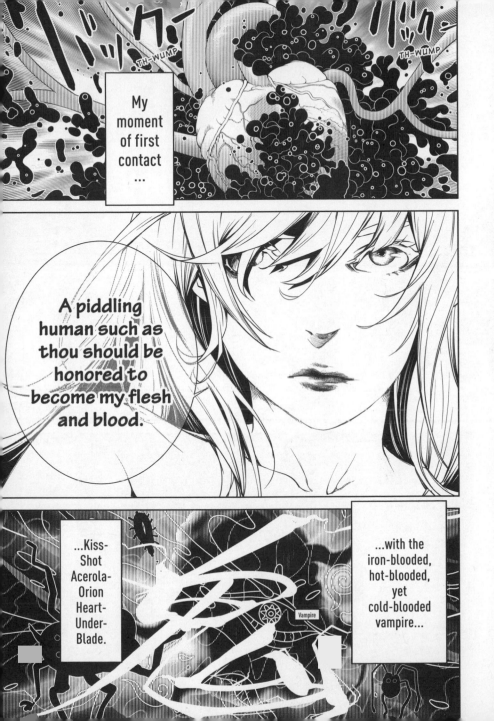

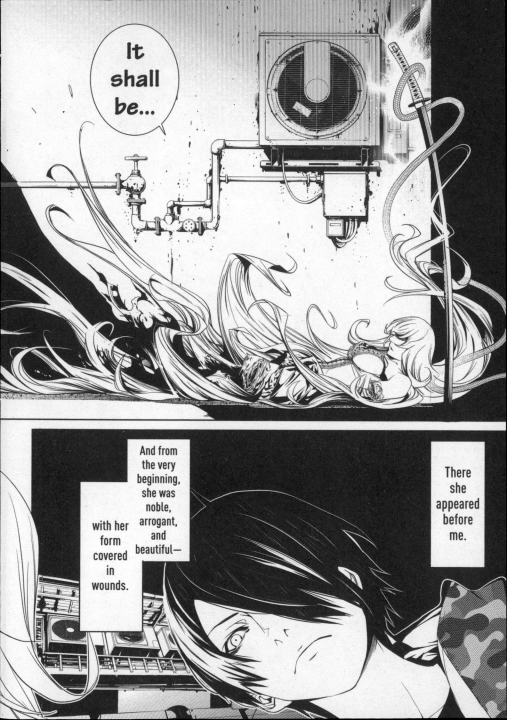

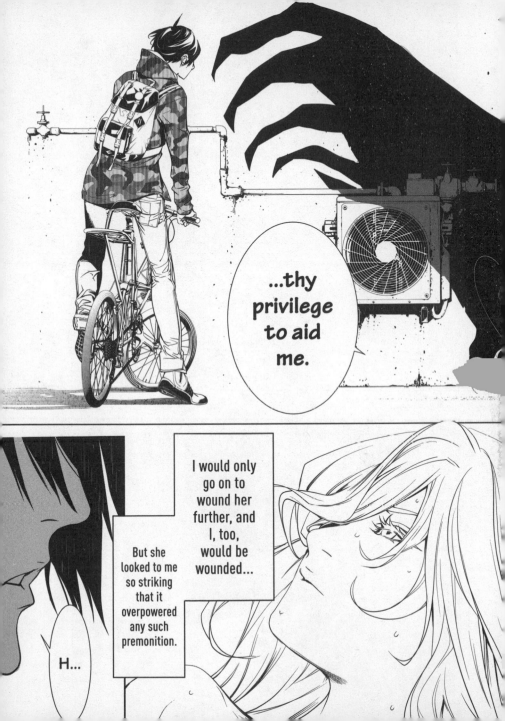

...thy privilege to aid me.

I would only go on to wound her further, and I, too, would be wounded...

But she looked to me so striking that it overpowered any such premonition.

H...

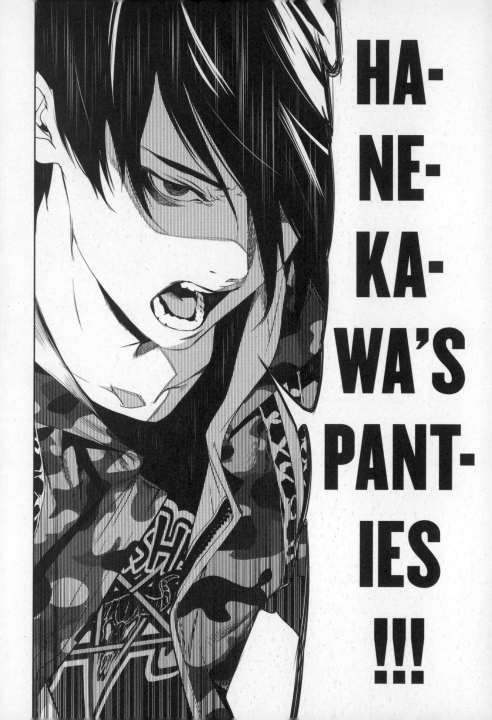

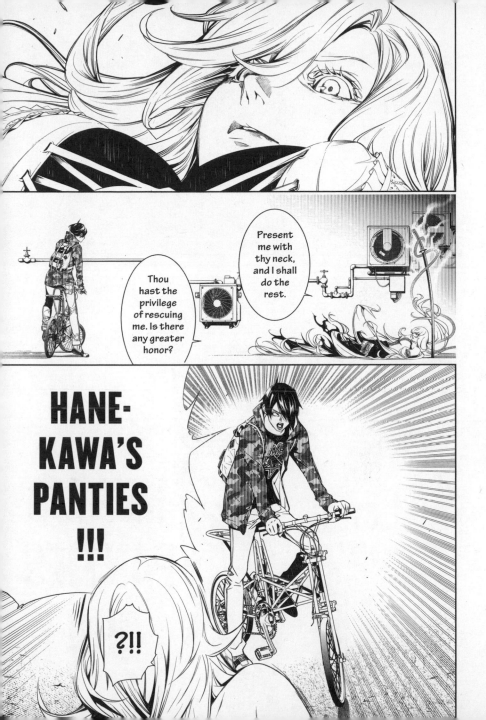

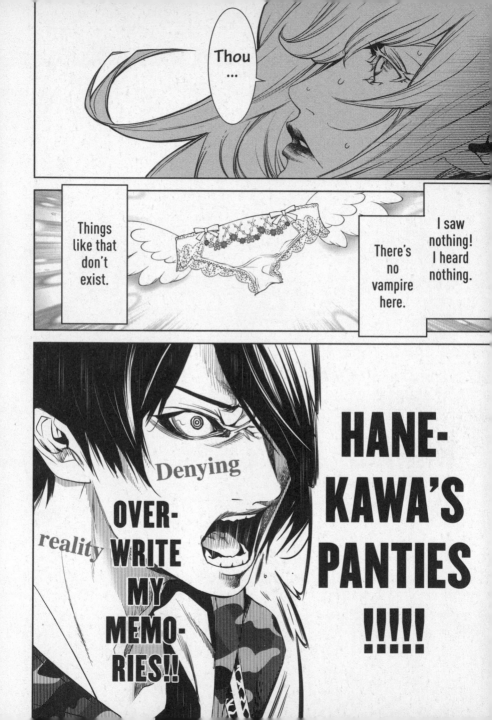

Continued in Volume 9

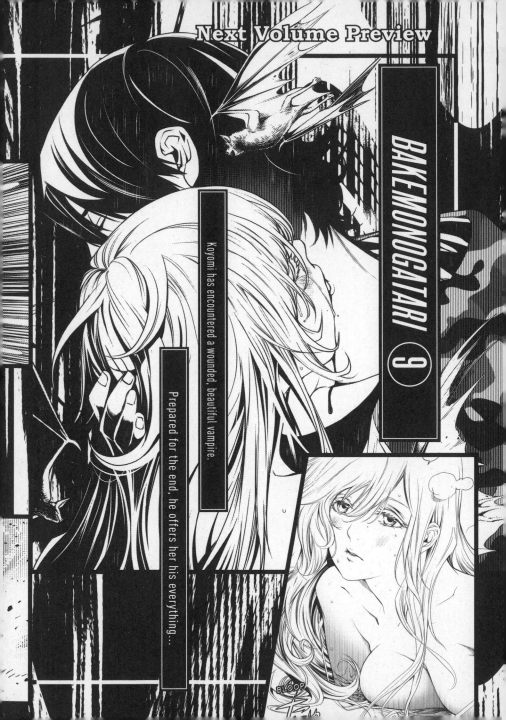

BAKEMONOGATARI 9

Koyomi has encountered a wounded, beautiful vampire.

Prepared for the end, he offers her his everything...